Blockchain & Decentralized Finance #1 Guide To Invest In Blockchain Technology, Cryptocurrencies, Altcoins, Smart Contracts and NFTs

Introduction

The DeFi movement is a response to the 2008 financial crisis and its aftermath. Even though its inception started many years ago, DeFi is a new concept in the world of finance. It is a part of the broader crypto-economy and has been gaining traction in recent times.

The DeFi movement is a new way to invest, borrow, and lend money without relying on any centralized institution like banks or governments. It relies on peer-to-peer lending, which means that loans, for instance, are not given by banks but by other individuals who are willing to offer them. Similarly, payments for goods and services can be made using cryptocurrencies instead of fiat currencies such as US dollars (USD) or euros (EUR). This way, no bank is needed to process those transactions.

DeFi pursues the decentralization of the power of finance and giving it back to the people.

The beginning of DeFi can be traced to 2008 when Satoshi Nakamoto, an anonymous person or a group of people experienced in cryptography, published a paper titled Bitcoin: A Peer-to-Peer Electronic Cash System. This paper introduced blockchain technology and the first-ever blockchain application, which was a form of digital currency that could not be manipulated by any single entity and was completely decentralized. Nakamoto named it 'Bitcoin'.

The introduction of Bitcoin in 2008 led to the creation of many other cryptocurrencies. These many other cryptocurrencies that have emerged are collectively known as 'altcoins' (defined as all cryptocurrencies different from Bitcoin). Ethereum and Litecoin are examples of altcoins that are now being used all around the world as a form of payment for goods and services.

The importance of the Nakamoto paper was that it was the first time anyone had come up with a way of transferring value without relying on centralized authorities like governments or banks.

1. Decentralized Finance

The finance sector is at a crossroads where it needs to evolve or become obsolete. It has been abundantly clear for years that the traditional centralized finance system is dying. Banks are struggling to adapt to the rapidly changing environment, and are being challenged by new players in their industry. The whole economic world order is in need of change.

Decentralized finance (DeFi) offers a better alternative to the centralized finance system by distributing power back into the hands of its users. DeFi is an emerging ecosystem that provides users with an abundant variety of financial products and services outside traditional systems. It is being seen as the next generation of the financial system.

DeFi is built on top of blockchain technology and it can be used to provide more transparency, security, and privacy for all participants in the decentralized economy.

The term DeFi was created in 2018 by a group of developers looking to work on financial applications outside of the traditional system. If you pay attention, the word DeFi has a subliminal meaning, sounding like the word 'defy'. That is the true intention of this system: the purpose behind DeFi is to defy the centralized financial system that we have today. The proponents wanted to show that they are not going to follow the old rules of finance and that they will be creating their own rules instead.

The current centralized banking system is flawed and does not work for our society. DeFi proposes an ecosystem where people can borrow and lend in crypto, without the need for a bank or central entity to manage the process.

How Does the Process Work?

In the beginning, DeFi was mainly used for crypto-backed lending platforms, crypto-backed exchanges, and decentralized hedge funds. Today, there are more than a hundred DeFi projects out there with different use cases—from tokenized fiat currencies to tokenized stocks.

A decentralized financial system does not have one single centralized authority, but instead relies on a distributed ledger to keep track of transactions. The ledger records all transactions in chronological order, creating an immutable record for everyone to see. This helps create trust among parties because it eliminates the need for a trusted third party to oversee the transaction.

Since the idea behind DeFi is to take the middleman out of financial transactions and give more power to the people, what happens is that instead of having your bank manage your money, you would hold it in a wallet on a blockchain and use smart contracts to make transactions with other people.

DeFi is mainly based on Ethereum, the next-most-popular cryptocurrency after Bitcoin. It is worth noting that DeFi is an umbrella term that encompasses all decentralized financial applications and protocols.

The main principles of DeFi are:

- a decentralized ecosystem for finance;
- open, transparent, and immutable records; and
- peer-to-peer transactions without intermediaries.

The key differentiating factor between the DeFi system and the traditional system is the power that participants have through smart contracts.

A smart contract is a tiny computer program that contains the terms of an agreement between a buyer and seller. When the smart contract executes, the transaction takes place and the details are recorded on the blockchain ledger. The process of creating a smart contract is relatively straightforward. It is just a matter of writing the code that will govern the terms of your agreement. You can then upload the code to an Ethereum-based blockchain, which not only stores it but also executes it.

The most popular use cases for DeFi are tokenizing assets and issuing tokens to represent shares in a company. These tokens can be traded on cryptocurrency exchanges and can be used as collateral for loans on decentralized exchanges.

Smart Contracts

In simple terms, a smart contract is a computer program that executes the terms of a contract automatically. The security of smart contracts has come a long way since their inception and they are now considered to be more secure than traditional transactions.

The concept of smart contracts was first introduced by Nick Szabo, an American computer scientist, in 1994 but it wasn't until 2008 that they were implemented into blockchain technology.

The security of smart contracts is an important issue. The Ethereum community has been working hard to ensure that the blockchain ecosystem is safe and secure. It is being improved with the help of blockchain technology and artificial intelligence. This technology can be applied in various ways to improve the security and transparency of smart contracts.

They are used in a wide variety of industries like finance, real estate, insurance, and more, and can be used in many different ways like creating digital assets, transferring ownership, or even voting.

Smart contracts have many benefits for both parties involved in a transaction. One of the main benefits is that they reduce the risk of fraud or financial loss by eliminating intermediaries such as lawyers and bankers. They also help prevent disputes and disagreements over terms.

Smart contracts are a type of computer code that is written on the blockchain's decentralized ledger and they allow the automatic execution of contractual agreements. This reduces the need for trust and intermediaries in business transactions. They also make it possible to transfer assets across borders without any third party involvement.

It is expected that smart contracts will grow in popularity as they become more mainstream and accepted by businesses. However, smart contracts have a number of limitations and there are some things that they can't do currently, which prevents them from reaching their full potential.

The most common limitation is that smart contracts can't be trusted. They are not governed by humans and there is no one to answer to if things go wrong. The code cannot be changed once it is published on the blockchain. So any error, no matter how small, is irreversible.

Another limitation of smart contracts is that they are not and can never be 100% secure. They can be hacked just like any other digital system and the consequences could be disastrous for those who were relying on them for their transactions.

Although the idea is that a smart contract is an automated and self-executing agreement between two or more parties, the reality is that it is difficult to verify if all parties have agreed to it or not. Furthermore, a smart contract may not be legally binding in all cases and they cannot cover every situation in which parties need arbitration, precisely because they are executed automatically without a third-party arbitrator.

In order to make sure that the contract is executed as intended, it is necessary for the parties involved to trust each other and trust the smart contract itself. This requires a lot of oversight from humans who will ensure that the terms of the contract are followed.

Smart contracts are not perfect and they cannot eliminate third-party involvement completely. They can only eliminate it partially, which means that there will always be some form of human intervention required for them to work as intended.

Smart contracts still need improvement and refinement before major players will trust them enough to obtain the benefits they promise.

What You Can Do With DeFi

The ecosystem of DeFi has grown exponentially since its inception. There are hundreds of projects in the space, with new ones being created every day.

Let's look at some of the most important services you can access through DeFi.

- Sending money around the world: One of the most popular DeFi services is MakerDAO, which allows people to send money anywhere in the world without having to worry about currency exchange rates or exchange fees.

- Global money flow: This is one of the most innovative uses for DeFi, which makes it an exciting space to explore. These are some ways it can make your life easier:

- You can create a stablecoin that is pegged to an asset or basket of assets.

- You can create a token that pays dividends from company profits or pays interest on loans given by people who have lent you money.

- You can create a token that gives you access to an exclusive community or club, such as live music events or even just a chat with friends about this particular event.

- Gain access to stable currencies: The ultimate goal of DeFi is to provide people with access to stable currencies like dollars or euros so they can invest, borrow, and lend without having to worry about the volatility of cryptocurrencies or their own national fiat currency.

- Funds can be borrowed with collateral: Borrowing funds with collateral through DeFi starts by putting up your assets as collateral, then releasing them when you repay the loan, just like a traditional bank loan. This tool can be used by anyone who wants to borrow money without having to go through banks or any other traditional financial institutions.

- Make crypto savings: With DeFi popular projects like MakerDAO and Compound, you are able to store your crypto assets and earn interest on them without having to go through traditional banking. A crypto saver can buy a tokenized asset, such as treasury bonds or stocks, which are backed by crypto assets like Bitcoin or Ether. They can also use the tokenized asset as collateral for borrowing money in order to invest in other tokens or cryptocurrencies.

- Trading tokens: DeFi allows users to trade tokens without any middleman taking a cut of their profits. There are also lending services, like the above-mentioned MakerDAO and Compound, that allow people to lend their crypto wealth and generate interest profit with it.

- Develop your portfolio: A portfolio is a collection of investments, loans, and trades. The most common portfolio is an investment portfolio. It consists of various types of investments, such as stocks or bonds. You can invest in DeFi through various platforms, such as decentralized exchanges, wallets, or even apps that are specifically designed for investing in DeFi. This way, you can diversify your investment portfolio by investing in different projects that you think are likely to succeed. The goal is to maximize the return on your money while minimizing the risk that you will lose it all.

- Keep track of your portfolio: The idea behind DeFi is to help people invest their money in ways that are more beneficial for them. There are many different ways that you can use decentralized financial tools, but the most common one is to manage your portfolio with decentralized exchanges. However, keeping track of your investments can be a daunting task. Fortunately, a host of products and services are prepared to help you. Online platforms like Personal Capital and Mint give you access to all your financial information in one place. You can set up various budgets and track any changes to your investments, loans, and trades.

- Finance your ideas: DeFi is a new way to fund your ideas without the need for traditional investors, banks, or venture capitalists. It is a decentralized financial system that allows people to invest in projects they are interested in and get returns.

- Purchase insurance: With DeFi, people can buy insurance for their homes and cars. This is a great way to get coverage without the high costs that come with traditional insurance companies. DeFi is a new way for people to get access to financial services without the need of a bank account or credit score. It is also more affordable than traditional banks and credit cards.

2. Introduction to Blockchain Technology

The first term you'll hear when delving into the world of cryptocurrencies is "blockchain." To understand Bitcoin, cryptocurrencies in general, and the future of decentralized computing, it is critical to understand the principles of blockchain technology.

The blockchain is the framework, or "protocol," on which Bitcoin functions, as well as many other cryptocurrencies and emerging technologies. Blockchain can be termed as a public ledger that is distributed across many computers throughout the world. Each Bitcoin transaction that happens is recorded and added to the blockchain as a new "block" and also linked to the previous transaction with a special timestamp, like a link in a long "chain."

Blockchain Uses

Blockchain has proven to be helpful and, above all, revolutionary in various industries. The first of all in finance, but it has also entered the world of medicine, insurance, or education very hard. With the following examples, you will see how Blockchain is changing the world as we know it:

Blockchain in the Insurance Industry

In not long, data storage using Blockchain technology in the insurance industry will become the new standard. This technology's high security and the ability to eliminate fraud and redundancy of policy information makes blockchain the natural choice for the insurance industry.

One of the most exciting points of blockchain technology is the possibility of generating Smart Contracts that could automatically approve or reject any claim for an insurance policy.

Blockchain in Finance/Banking

Indeed, the most popular applications are in this sector since blockchain technology can manage many processes that will truly revolutionize banking as we know it. Here you can read an excellent excerpt from the essay on the evolution of finances by Alex Tapscott and Don Tapscott for the Harvard Business Review

As cryptocurrencies gain popularity, major economic powers such as China will take steps to adopt digital currency. In short, Blockchain can revolutionize our financial system and eliminate the need for so many intermediary companies, which only lengthen and make them more expensive.

Blockchain and Medicine

It helps manage data and automate processes in an industry where precision is a matter of life and death. In the US, a medical error is one of the most common causes of death. Storing records on a blockchain would reduce redundancies and errors that lead to those deaths. Blockchain also enables greater precision in pharmaceutical medication, which would help patients prevent the diversion of opiates to illegal markets.

Blockchain and Logistics

In the supply chains and logistics industries, blockchain makes it easier to track the location of commodities as they are produced, packaged, and distributed to various points of sale. Smart Contracts allow payments and authorizations to be made through the products' GPS location; this aspect would increase the efficiency in this industry for an approximate value of 1,500 million dollars.

Blockchain and Real Estate

In this industry, blockchain is increasing the efficiency of real estate transactions, reducing the time it takes to check the financial information of each of those involved, thus improving transparency in the industry. All of this would help make document forgeries or rental scams virtually impossible, rendering all property-related transactions incorruptible.

Blockchain and Education

In education, blockchain technology will help standardize the verification of certificates issued by learning institutions. It can also be guaranteed that all educators' credentials are valid. Redundancies would be eliminated, and errors in student performance data would be avoided.

Blockchain in Marketing

The applications, in this case, are very diverse, and therefore, the industry will improve precision when choosing its target consumers. For the benefit of consumers themselves, transparency will increase considerably.

Blockchain will ensure that people are not overexposed to certain advertising pieces or even get people automatically paid for using their data. It will be possible to verify that the followers of a brand are people and not bots. The legitimacy of sponsored contests can be guaranteed, ensuring only one vote per participant.

Blockchain and Business

As you can imagine, the applications of blockchain technology in business are infinite, from improving the accuracy or transparency of records to eliminating administrative processes that ultimately hinder efficiency. There is a long way to go to discover and, above all, to optimize. But financial experts are completely confident that we will see full adoption of this technology in industries in no time.

Blockchain Myths

Since blockchain still does not make sense to everyone, there are going to be myths that float around about the technology and the cryptocurrency that is used on it. Most of these tales are going to cause people to do not want to invest in blockchain because they are scared to do so. Some of these myths can be debunked and put your mind at rest about blockchain and hopefully make it to where you are going to want to invest with blockchain because you understand it just a little bit better.

Blockchain Is Decentralized and Can Split Itself Off From Bitcoin

Depending on who you talk to is going to end up depending on what you hear about bitcoin and if it is a currency that has been successful or has failed. As you look at the same line, these people are going to end up saying that blockchain is isolated and can be rebuilt on a transaction system that is decentralized. However, this is not true!

When you look at reality, it is going to show you that blockchain is already strongly decentralized, and this is because of the encryption that is offered on the system because of the algorithms and protocols that are set up on the network so that miners can determine if they should validate a transaction or not.

Other bitcoin platforms such as ethereum are developing their own blockchain that is going to be similar to the bitcoin blockchain. However, since etherum is still brand new, it is always evolving to meet the needs of its users while keeping the system decentralized.

Tens of Thousands of Merchants Are Using Bitcoin

Having that many people using bitcoin would be amazing! But, sadly, there are not very many merchants out there that are going to accept bitcoin for payment. There is only around eighty percent of cryptocurrency being used for hoarding instead of actual spending. So, if a merchant allows you to use cryptocurrency to pay for a good or service, then they are going to be letting you use them in a facility that is their partner, which means that they are going to take the digital currency and turn it into actual money so that they can use it to buy things that need to be purchased to keep their business running. But, there are going to be risks and fees that are put in place when you are the merchant accepting cryptocurrency.

There are a few merchants that are accepting cryptocurrency and are testing the waters to see how it works and if it is a practical process for a business to use. Most of the merchants that are accepting cryptocurrency are doing so to get media exposure and more customers in their doors.

The Transactions Are Going to Be Processed in Real Time Like a Bank Handles Their Transactions

Incorrect! There is a ten-minute delay between when a transaction is processed on the blockchain. Therefore, two transactions are going to be completed per second with bitcoin.

Transactions That Are Done on Bitcoin Are "Almost Free"

Once again, this is wrong! There is going to be a processing fee that is going to come with using bitcoin, but it is not going to be charged to the users or the merchants. The people who are using blockchain to mine are going to process the transaction, which is going to be ninety-nine percent of the revenue that a miner makes. Therefore, this is going to come to around twenty-one million bitcoins that are mined, which is estimated to happen approximately 2140. But, once that occurs, there is no set plan that is going to tell people what the transaction costs are going to be.

These transactions are going to be processed and will reward minimally through the network with a small portion of bitcoins. This is not the representation of the actual revenue that a miner is going to receive. Most miner rewards are going to end up justifying the high costs that are associated with the transaction.

Exchange commissions added up all of the costs, and sooner rather than later there are not going to be any negligible costs that are in the system.

Bitcoin Has the Most Secure Currencies

While this is true because bitcoin holds a high resilience to attacks, it is just like any other transaction system that is going to have breaches in security because of human error or fraud.

In 2015 alone there were:

- Three hundred and eighty-seven million dollars in fraud by clients that vanished from a bitcoin exchange in Hong Kong.
- Thanks to a phishing attack, two million dollars in bitcoin were lost.
- The bitcoin exchange in Canada was shut down because someone compromised their database.

And trading was temporarily suspended because of one wallet that is in operation was compromised, thus compromising the entire system.

Bitcoin's Ecosystem Is Decentralized

Mining pools on the blockchain have increased. But, at least one of the top four mining pools is in China on their exchange. The bigger mining pools are going to be artificially limited so that democracy does not show any favoritism. But, those that work with a smaller pool are going to be pushed out of business because of the larger ones. It is just like any system where the bigger you are, the more money you are going to end up being able to spend on controlling the market.

One of the reasons behind the dominance is because bitcoins are going to be generated through mining, and that is becoming harder because the number of coins in the system has increased. And, the more prominent mining farms are going to have the money that is needed to invest and operate their farms while other farms are being shut down because of the high operating costs.

There are a few opaque players that have been controlling the system, and this allows for the system to modify the transaction rules, which ends up making it harder for others to get into the investments due to the fact that they cannot keep up with the protocols that are changing all of the time.

You should think back to school when there was a bully and they were losing a game. And, because they keep losing the game, they do not want to show that they are missing and therefore the rules continue to change so that they can win in the end. While this does not seem fair, you are not going to be able to argue with the bully on the rules because they are going to be bigger and end up hurting you in the long run. This is the same with the big farms. Because they have more money, they are going to be able to use their money and end up causing you to go out of business. This is why it is easier to just go with the flow and the rules that are continually changing instead of arguing with them.

Bitcoin Is Idealistic and Non-Profit

There are millions of dollars being invested in bitcoin. It has already been around five billion dollars that have been accumulated into the bitcoin system, which was used to get the system up and running. On top of that, there are going to be billions of dollars that are invested in bitcoin wallets, exchanges, and miner operations. Examples that show that:

- Coinbase has raised one hundred million dollars to be used in blockchain operations.
- Fifty million dollars was invested by Circle, which is a Goldman Sachs startup.

- One hundred and sixteen million dollars was raised by VC in Silicon Valley so that a stealth mode could be placed on the blockchain.

Blockchain Is Secure

There are features that are going to be put into place for the writing of data due to the fact that there has to be Proof of Work on the blockchain. Blocks are going to be added to the chain whenever a transaction has been validated to make sure there are no double calculations being placed on the chain. Since the blocks on the blockchain are going to be able to be used by all the users, it is going to be expensive if you attempt to mine your own chain.

There are going to be private blockchains where there will be mechanisms that have to be replaced for the proof of the work, which causes there to be a limit on the things that other people can add to the chain that is created. In other words, block validators will end up being built.

The rules have made it to where blocks are going to be specified by a signed list of signatories. This list is going to be limited so that the system can make sure that the entries take turns writing blocks so that there are enough to go around. Bad behavior is highly discouraged and will limit because of the round-robin style of work.

Blockchain Is Encrypted

There are different cryptographic methods that bitcoins use along with the data that is going to be encrypted and placed on the blockchain. Because of this, a lot of people believe that all of the information that is put on the blockchain is encrypted, but this is not true.

Most of the data that is located on the blockchain is going to be unencrypted since the information does not need to be validated. This is because there is not going to be any way to unencrypt the information that is supposed to be approved.

Whenever you are using a private blockchain, the nodes are going to be able to decrypt the data through decryption keys. But, if you are going to do this, then you are going to know why you're trying to encrypt the data in the first place.

There has been researching done with cryptography and solutions have been revealed showing that the data that does not have any underlying evidence is going to have no knowledge of proof. So, whenever you look at this technology, you will come to realize that it is not as mature as it appears to be.

Privacy is vitally important to everyone, but why would you want to encrypt the data that is on the blockchain? If the information is in motion, should it be encrypted? The information that is resting, does that need to be encoded? And finally, when the data has been encrypted, who is going to have access to it? When should it be decrypted? When should someone's permission be revoked so that they no longer have access to the data?

Management of the data is going to be critical of the security for the data that is on the server. When should the information be shared freely between two different parties? You need to carefully consider the security of the data that is on the blockchain to find a solution that will help protect what needs to be protected while still allowing the nodes to validate the information.

3. Blockchain Economy Design Principles

Much of decentralization focuses on the impact it will have on our monetary systems. As such, the term blockchain economy is gaining popularity. What does this mean, though? In short, it refers to apps and systems that are designed with decentralization in mind and do not incorporate any form of centralized control.

Financial applications offer a great testbed for decentralized apps because finance manages to gather many of the real-world obstacles that decentralization faces in other applications. It's no coincidence that one of the first applications to be launched was Bitcoin. What better way to test drive the usability of a decentralized app than to launch a currency?

As such, Bitcoin has been improved upon by other cryptocurrencies. Examining the way they work is instructive because it provides lessons on how decentralization works and the principles that govern its design.

Design Principles

There are seven principles that all blockchain designs rely on. No matter a network's rules and protocols, you'll find these principles in every decentralized app. These principles derive from the problems that arise from centralized platforms. The most interesting aspect of these principles is how Bitcoin incorporated all of them before there was any discussion of them.

What I mean is, Bitcoin managed to organically incorporate all of these principles without the need for improvements or iterations. In contrast, if you look at the typical development cycle for a piece of software, it goes through multiple iterations until it arrives at a production-ready state. In Bitcoin's case, it came fully equipped out of the box.

That highlights the blockchain's strength as a solution and the ease with which other developers can create applications on it.

The First Principle

The first principle that the blockchain incorporates is network integrity. That feature has everything to do with trust and the transparency of interactions taking place on it. Before Bitcoin launched, there was no network where actions were fully trustworthy. For instance, consider a common financial transaction on the internet. It's hard to establish trust when buying something online. It's so hard that you have to share mountains of data with firms like Amazon to complete a transaction. Essentially, you don't have a choice.

When it comes to money, there is a unique problem from an integrity perspective. Money isn't data. Data can be replicated and shared in multiple formats. For instance, if you record a video, you can send it to multiple people without hesitation. The network doesn't lose integrity because the video is the same no matter who consumes it.

However, money doesn't work the same way. You cannot send a dollar to your friend and send that same dollar to someone else. Money is finite and isn't replicable. Try to pay someone with non-existent money, and you'll find yourself running a Ponzi scheme. When you transact online, you have to place your trust in some central authority to ensure there isn't any double-spending going on. Institutions like banks, card issuers, and large merchant platforms assume this role, but it comes at a high cost.

Decentralized currency networks like Bitcoin have to solve this double-spend problem to establish trust. The way Bitcoin does it is by establishing a consensus mechanism. The best part is that a decentralized consensus mechanism works far better than a central authority. Here's how Bitcoin's consensus algorithm works.

Every spend and transaction on the network is time-stamped and thus, subsequent spends of the same coin by the same user are rejected. Miners, who are network participants running nodes, gather recent transactions and create blocks out of them. This process occurs every 10 minutes. As I mentioned previously, each block contains a hash that refers to the preceding block. Without the hash, a block is invalid.

The Bitcoin blockchain is public, which means everyone can view transactions taking place. In essence, Bitcoin transactions are more traceable and transparent than cash. From a technical standpoint, the consensus algorithm is a seemingly complex one. Don't worry. I'm not going to bore you with jargon.

Bitcoin's consensus algorithm is named Proof of Work and it's a simple yet powerful algorithm. On Bitcoin's network, no user can select the identity of the miner that creates the latest block. Instead, it's a merit-based process where miners have to compete for the right to do so. The reward is doled out by having miners solve a cryptographic puzzle that is hard to solve but easy to verify.

Whoever solves the problem the quickest gets to create the next block. In solving the puzzle, miners expend computing hardware and electricity. The puzzle itself involves deciphering the next block's hash. Once the puzzle is solved, Bitcoin is awarded to the miner. Its cryptographic roots assure no shortcuts or ways to game the system when solving for an answer.

Thus, when an answer is produced, the entire network trusts it because everyone knows the work that went into solving the problem. Also, note that the puzzle-solving process is a constant one. It isn't as if a bell rings every 10 minutes and everyone starts figuring out puzzles. Over 500,000 trillion hashes are being deciphered every second. It's just that the likelihood of a hash being solved is 10 minutes.

Some miners might take a minute while others might take an hour. Solving the problem itself is an iterative process with miners making a variety of inputs and trying to match the output to what the network expects. The expected hash value is set by the network and is adjusted every 2,016 blocks. If the miner's output is incorrect, they adjust their inputs and try once again.

Currently, the number of hash attempts on the Bitcoin network is over 700 million trillion. That's a ton of resources spent on solving hashes to earn a Bitcoin. As you can see, there are some shortcomings to the proof of work consensus mechanism. It prioritizes miners who have the most firepower. The more powerful your computer is, the greater are your chances of earning Bitcoin.

Proof of work also exposes the network to manipulation. Let's say a group of miners who represent 51% of the network decide to band together and mine coins in tandem. The majority of coins generated from that point onwards would belong to those miners, and they would control the network. At that point, decentralization doesn't exist anymore. Naturally, trust erodes in such an environment.

In a bid to avoid such a calamity, alternatives emerged. Ethereum is the second most popular cryptocurrency, and its first version used the proof of work mechanism. However, Ethereum 1.1 replaced proof of work with proof of stake. Proof of stake requires miners to invest in the network and have current ownership of coins to participate.

Voting on the blockchain doesn't require heavy firepower as a result, and only those who are invested in the network and have spent time and resources developing it get to have a say in its propagation. It's a fairer system of determining who gets rewarded. It avoids the issue of someone entering the network with an arsenal of computers and overtaking existing miners. It removes any incentive for an arms race.

There are other consensus mechanisms out there. Ripple and Stellar use social networks to build consensus and require new entrants to generate at least 100 nodes before gaining the right to vote on a transaction. Essentially, this is the proof of work algorithm with some social media thrown into it. Social engineers and trolls can manipulate it. It automatically favors someone famous and as such, it isn't a very good model.

Another mechanism is titled proof of activity. This protocol combines proof of work and proof of stake. A random selection of miners signs off on a block by solving its hash before it's added to the network. A list of miners who have been pre-qualified using the proof of work and stake algorithms makes up the selection. The downside of this consensus mechanism is that transaction times take a while to complete.

Currently, Bitcoin's average transaction time is 10 minutes which is interminably long. This mechanism takes even longer since so much depends on the list of miners reaching consensus. Imagine standing in line to pay for something using Bitcoin and having to wait 10 minutes or more to confirm payment.

Proof of storage and proof of capacity are alternative consensus mechanisms. Both require miners to allocate a significant portion of their hard drive to mining or a significant portion of their shared disk space if they're operating in the cloud. How do these mechanisms help build network integrity?

Storage on a blockchain is an important function. When we think of data storage, we usually think of the way data is stored on the internet. Think of an article published on BuzzFeed or some other clickbait website. The article is up for a long time, but it's consumed and referred to for a relatively short time. Eventually, it gets lost in the recesses of storage. It's time-stamped, but its time of publication isn't important to the network it exists on.

After all, a new article published after it doesn't derive any meaning from the original date of publication. If you fail to notice a timestamp on a humorous article, you're not going to immediately swear off the website. However, data on a blockchain functions differently, as does storage.

Returning to the Bitcoin blockchain, a single coin cannot be used multiple times. That means it has to reference its history and the history of the blockchain. That is why the timestamp is so important. Before approving a transaction, the coin has to provide the network the history of the total number of coins that existed (to make sure coins haven't magically appeared or disappeared) and that the coin isn't existing doubly in someone else's wallet (to prevent double-spending).

That calls for a lot of storage space, and thus, the amount of storage a miner dedicates to the network is a good indicator of the trust they can bring to it. The more storage a blockchain network has to call upon, the more trustworthy it is. Thus, it makes sense to value storage and reward those who contribute a lot of it. The problem is that these algorithms are proof of work, rebranded.

They turn storage into the subject of an arms race instead of computing power. As such, there are limitations here as well. However, these mechanisms are the best that we have right now. The future will undoubtedly give us even more mechanisms. Currently, proof of stake is perhaps the best solution, but it disadvantages new entrants, which justifies the existence of alternative mechanisms.

Whatever the limitations of these mechanisms might be, there's no doubt that establishing trust is simple in a decentralized network. The entire peer network takes part in establishing it, and it isn't left to some centralized authority to determine what passes and what fails. The result is that we don't need the traditional central authorities like a central bank or retail banks to govern the flow of money.

As our world becomes increasingly digital, establishing trust online has become more important than ever. The blockchain's consensus mechanisms help establish trust and create lasting changes in our societies.

The Second Principle

The blockchain's second principle is that of distributed or democratized power. It's a well-established fact that the best form of governance is a democracy. It isn't perfect, but systems work better in the long run when everyone affected by it has a say in how it's run. Computer network architecture has never followed this pattern.

Instead, most network architecture has resembled a monarchy where a single authoritarian controls everything. While decisions are made faster in such network designs, they also open it to a single point of failure. Attack the central authority or subjugate it, and you control the whole network.

Blockchain distributes network power across every participant. There is no single point of control, and neither can any single party shut the system down. If a portion of the system is isolated or cut off from the rest, it isn't an issue since the blockchain's record is maintained by every node in the network. Thus, once the isolated nodes come back online, they fit back in seamlessly.

The only vulnerability is when a majority of malicious nodes take over the entire system and try to manipulate it. While such attacks cannot be fully prevented, they can be spotted from a mile away since every other node will receive a copy of the transactions in the network. Thus, decentralized power exists for longer and in safer hands.

One of the reasons we need decentralized systems is because internet giants have repeatedly violated the social contract they have with their users. They've used private assets to get wealthy and have used them without permission. They're unlikely to ever face any penalty for doing so. Governments are no better, using the internet to spy on their citizens and use personal data against them.

Worst of all, these centralized institutions spend billions of dollars each year securing themselves, but their inherent flaw never disappears. All of them continue to have a single point of failure and continue to provide attackers an incentive to test their defenses.

Blockchain revolutionizes this picture because there is no need for cybersecurity when the network itself is secure. Overpowering the blockchain requires more resources than rewards can compensate attackers with. What's more, the Bitcoin blockchain (and every other public blockchain) embraces a concept called bootstrapping. That isn't bootstrapping in the business sense.

In blockchain terms, bootstrapping refers to any user's ability to download the Bitcoin client onto their local machine and participate in the network. It's distributed across a volunteer network and rests on millions of computers worldwide simultaneously. The result is that attackers can never disable or isolate the network.

Governments and authoritarian heads of state cannot control the flow of money through executive orders. Currently, governments control the flow of money by squeezing bank accounts. Banks, for their part, don't enforce citizen's rights as much as question why citizens need rights in the first place. Blockchain removes the middleman and thus removes the bottleneck to a democratized system completely.

Best of all, the network's rules are simple, and coin creation is transparent. A coin is a reward provided to miners who manage to solve the crypto puzzle and add a new block to the network. The entire network gets to view the proof of work, and there are no doubts about the veracity of a transaction.

No Federal Reserve is turning the supply of money on and off as they wish. There are no banks conducting compliance checks to control the flow of money. It gives every user on the network full control of their assets and creates a robust network that is almost impossible to hack or compromise.

The Third Principle

One of the curious things about centralized systems is that the incentive system is all wrong. Let's take a bank, for instance. Banks make money from the interest they earn on loans. People who have good credit scores and can make payments on time typically receive low interest rates as an incentive to sign up for a loan. However, there are only so many people with good credit, and every bank competes for their attention.

As a result of this system, two outcomes take place. The first is that banks that market their services well capture the lion's share of the good customers and ignore the rest. That means those with poor or no credit, such as students, get ignored. These are the very people who need financial assistance, but most banks don't lend money to them.

That brings us to the second outcome. The less successful banks prey on these people and offer them credit cards and other costly loans with high interest rates. These loans are often packaged as credit builder loans or adjustable-rate or zero-down loans. The bottom line with all of them is a high interest rate that boosts bank profits.

Short-term incentives such as these lead to more defaults and a perennial debt cycle for the middle and lower classes. In turn, this widens the income inequality in society which fuels social unrest. That is the cycle that created the 2008 financial crisis, and it continues to this day.

The blockchain and Bitcoin's network sought to repair this system by realigning incentives. First, distributed power removes any incentive for attackers to compromise the system. Thus, security came built-in. Next, the proof of work consensus system rewards those who take part in the system and nurture it. The earliest miners on the Bitcoin network received 50 BTC for every node they verified.

That was the reward offered during the first three years of BTC's existence. This reward size didn't remain consistent. The reward size was decreased to incentivize further long-term participation and widespread adoption. After all, as BTC grew more popular, the network had to make sure that the earliest and most loyal adopters were rewarded well.

This message resonated with later adopters since they understood that the earlier someone adopted BTC, the more they'd be rewarded. However, there was danger lurking here. If people kept adopting BTC, inflation would eventually strike. The value of BTC would diverge from its price since supply would be unlimited.

To counter this, Nakamoto placed a cap on the number of BTC that could be mined on the network. According to current mining rates, the final BTC will be mined in 2041. The Limited supply gives inherent value to every coin, and as a result, inflation is countered.

The bottom line of all of these features is everyone is incentivized to play by the network's rules and assist each other in increasing the democratization of the network. There's nothing to be gained by preying on someone else, and no authority can ever take over the network. Everyone benefits when users share the benefits. Thus, incentives are in line with network propagation.

These features have significant implications beyond currencies. What if smart contracts securing proof of assets could be stored on the blockchain? What if property and land records could be stored? The entire economic system would incentivize itself for everyone's mutual benefit. There wouldn't be any preying on the underserved or vulnerable sections of society.

The blockchain would also eliminate middlemen who collect rent from our activities. Given the advances in the internet of things, what if payments could be handled in Bitcoin (or any cryptocurrency) from one IT device to another without the need to convert money between multiple fiat currencies and pay a gate fee to intermediaries?

I mentioned previously that the blockchain represents a chance for our society to have a do-over with the internet. The initial internet era, call it Web 1.0, was a collaborative place where users contributed to its growth. The rise of Google, Facebook, Amazon, and Apple killed that, and these corporations took control of communications using stolen assets.

Centralized systems eventually get cannibalized by big corporations and entities. The field of artificial intelligence is currently having its transition moment from Web 1.0 to whatever came after that. Initial AI research was built on open-source libraries and collaboration. However, we're now starting to see commercial AI development where progress is walled off from the rest of the market and benefits a select few as they seek to dominate the marketplace.

That is impossible to execute on a blockchain since there's no incentive to do so. As a result, the network will always be decentralized and democratic.

The Fourth Principle

As with anything on the internet or any network for that matter, security is an extremely important feature. The internet, as it currently stands, is an extremely unsafe place. Cyberattacks, ransomware, malware, phishing attacks, and cyberbullying are common occurrences, and we spend significant resources protecting ourselves from their ill effects. When designing the Bitcoin blockchain, Satoshi Nakamoto engineered an almost foolproof cryptographic algorithm that leverages an age-old security concept.

It's called asymmetric cryptography, and it uses two keys to ensure security. One key handles encryption, and the other handles decryption, which explains the term asymmetric. The concept of asymmetric cryptography isn't new. It's been around since the 1970s. In cryptographic circles, using old algorithms is a good thing since they're tried and tested.

Unlike cybersecurity devices that have to keep evolving to stay abreast of attacks, cryptography algorithms that survive the test of time tend to be the most stable. New algorithms eventually get exposed by some little-known vulnerability. An algorithm that has existed for over 40 years has clearly withstood many attacks. It explains why the U.S Department of Defense is the only other network larger than the Bitcoin network to use this form of security.

In this system, the onus of security is on the user. They have to secure their private keys at all costs, and if they forget their keys, they cannot recover them. The information continues to exist on the blockchain but it's not accessible. No one else can access it without the private key either. The earlier days of Bitcoin saw users misunderstand this concept and trust their private keys to third parties.

The result was massive theft and loss of value. However, as time has moved on, knowledge has increased. The need to always secure a private key does open a vulnerability; therefore, cybersecurity isn't rendered totally obsolete. However, it is localized to a single device or piece of hardware that stores the key. As such it doesn't have to be exposed to the network and this minimizes the chances that it will be hacked.

Security is also tied to incentives and ends up as a by-product. Here's how it works. We know that the longest blockchain is the most secure since the resources needed to overpower it are too expensive. A chain grows longer only when users are active and keep adding blocks to it. In the Bitcoin blockchain, users are incentivized to add blocks as previously explained, and thus, as activity increases, the chain becomes longer and more secure.

As our world becomes more dependent on technology, adopting the blockchain for its security standards alone makes a ton of sense. Imagine a situation where a self-driving car is hacked by someone halfway across the world through a centralized network. What if missiles and other weapons were hijacked? Our world is interconnected, and distances have been reduced to nothing.

Centralized networks cannot provide full security because of their single point of failure. Attackers always know where to look. In contrast, attackers don't know where to begin with the blockchain, and even if they do, it takes a lot to overpower the system before the rest of the network fights back. Its simplicity ensures security.

Security isn't a principle of the network as much as it is a natural by-product. The only addition that decentralized applications like Bitcoin add, is the use of a cryptographic protocol to enhance security. Different networks use different protocols. Much like how consensus mechanisms differ, there is some debate about which protocol offers the best security.

For instance, Monero uses ring signatures that are slightly different from the asymmetric cryptography protocol Bitcoin uses. Ring signatures mask everything about a transaction and thus combine privacy and security into one bundle. Whichever protocol is used, there's no doubt that security is a guarantee on the blockchain.

The Fifth Principle

Big data has transformed businesses in every sector. Corporations collect more data than ever before. Simply accessing a website means providing the website's owner access to your IP address, where you live, your browsing habits, your preferences, and in some cases, your preferred third-party websites. When Google first introduced Google Analytics, it was an innocent enough project. Website owners could track what their visitors were seeing and use that to improve their sites. Google did this by installing a file called a cookie on the visitor's computer.

Then companies like Facebook and Amazon came along and turned the humble cookie into a cookie monster. Facebook was especially prolific in this area, installing cookies that tracked browser activity not just on Facebook but outside of it as well. If you visited a shopping website after visiting Facebook, the company knew about it. They tracked how much time you spent on that website, which pages you looked at, and what you hovered your mouse over, and for how long.

Google caught up quickly with these practices, and eventually, banner ads that followed you from one website to the next began appearing. In recent times, Apple has made a huge fuss about privacy, but in reality, all they've done is gate customer data away from the other big tech companies. That's why you've never been able to use Apple's products easily with other platforms and have to choose Apple's network to solve your issues.

Data is wealth these days, and data privacy is at the core of the blockchain's design. Every application built on it adheres to this principle, and it's impossible to erase it. Transactions carried out on Ethereum's blockchain (or any cryptocurrency) are private and crucially aren't identity-linked.

You can download the Ethereum client on your machine and start participating on it. You don't have to provide an email address or any other identification. When you transact on the network, your wallet (where you store your coins) is the only data available to the public.

That doesn't mean privacy is guaranteed. It is possible to triangulate data points in transactions and verify who owns a wallet. However, unlike centralized mechanisms, the blockchain's apps don't make it immediately obvious. The entire network is transaction-based, not identity-based.

That has both advantages and disadvantages. On one hand, you're assured that there isn't some government agent snooping on your transaction, building a data avatar of you. Think of it this way: If you use Google regularly, have an Android phone that tracks your location, visit websites that have Google Analytics enabled, and use Google Pay to pay for products and services, Google knows everything about you.

They know what you like, dislike, where you've been, what you ate yesterday, what clothes you like wearing, and even what your romantic life looks like. Substitute the word Google for Government, and everyone would be up in arms about this scenario. However, since a corporation is doing this and not a totalitarian government, we accept it passively. Governments do track us like this, and even democratic societies have turned into surveillance states where we have to prove that we don't need to be tracked instead of receiving our basic right of privacy as standard.

The blockchain flips this picture on its head and removes the surveillance aspect completely. People can share what they want to share and nothing else. If you want to share browsing habits with a trusted company, you can opt-in. Currently, you have to opt out of data sharing, which highlights how our privacy is disrespected.

The flip side of the privacy debate is that without identity-linked networks, crime would spread like wildfire. This argument is true. Bitcoin's early days were characterized by criminals laundering their cash using coins and evading taxes. As such, this doesn't help society, and no one would argue that money laundering is a price to pay for privacy.

However, it isn't as if identity-linked networks stop or eliminate financial crime either. There's a reason tax havens exist. Why should every person in society give up their right to privacy for the sake of combating a select few who engage in criminal activity? In the guise of monitoring criminal activity, banks and governments routinely overstep their boundaries and treat everyone as if they're guilty.

A good solution would be to combine decentralization with centralized networks. Currently, cryptocurrency exchanges work this way, even though they lean heavily towards centralization. Coinbase, for instance, requires users to prove their identity before granting access to their trading software. There's no earthly reason to do this other than to allow the government to track capital gains profits. However, the IRS mandates users file taxes on profits earned from cryptocurrencies. So why is there a dual-layer of centralization?

The bottom line is that the blockchain represents a massive step forward for privacy thanks to its design. We will need to design a framework that eliminates the need for identity tracking to the extremes it's currently taken to and prevent crime at the same time.

The Sixth Principle

Imagine you're running an eCommerce store selling products. A customer likes your product and pays for it via Paypal. You have an account with Paypal, and you receive the money. The problem is Paypal arbitrarily decides to hang onto your cash for 30 days because there have been instances of fraud previously. Instead of prosecuting fraudulent cases, they punish everyone by assuming ownership of their cash and only send it to you if you accept their terms and conditions. There's no way to fight the system, and customer service is non-existent.

That is a real scenario that online merchants face all the time. Banks aren't much better. Let's say you're running a business and suddenly land a major deal that's many figures greater than what you typically earn. The bank will freeze your account almost certainly until you can explain where the money comes from. Even if you do explain it adequately, you're at their mercy and depend on them to give you access to your cash. All of this is in the name of compliance. You're treated as a criminal and have to prove your innocence.

Centralized systems such as these trample all over our rights without a second thought. Paypal's user agreement famously specifies that their users waive the right to impose a class action lawsuit on the company by using their services. Such arrogance comes about only thanks to centralized systems. The blockchain adjusts this balance and gives people their rights back. In the examples above, rights are being stolen by incompetent middlemen whose services we need due to a lack of alternatives.

On a blockchain, there are no middlemen, and there's no possibility of such occurrences taking place. There's a larger picture of the rights issue. Let's say you're a filmmaker and create media. This media is then uploaded on Youtube by someone in its original format, and your film is now free for everyone to see, and you don't get a cent in return.

You can lease the rights to view the film (or artwork) to someone else in exchange for royalties, but why would anyone pay money for something that's free? As a result, trust words. Centralized platforms such as Youtube enforce creator's rights, but there is no end to pirated movie clips and songs on the platform. Besides, if Youtube can run ads on videos and earn money, this hardly aligns with the interests of the creators.

Even here, youtube absolves itself of all rights once the content is uploaded. If you think your content has been pirated, it's up to you to flag it as copyrighted content and have it taken down. Youtube decides whether your claim is true or not, and there's no way to appeal the decision. What gives Youtube the right to act as a judge? They're a middleman, nothing else. They don't create anything and yet assume all the power.

Social media platforms often behave this way and have humungous control over what information is disseminated. In the United States, you'll find right and left-wing extremists complaining about censorship and might think it's a good thing that extreme content is censored.

However, this isn't the case in other countries. For instance, India is a democratic country. Yet, the Indian government has never hesitated to push its agenda on social media and crackdown on dissent. Dissenting opinions are censored by platforms such as Facebook and Twitter, and even Google. Dissenters are prosecuted for contradicting the government, and social media companies couldn't care less because they get to continue with business as usual.

Middlemen get to decide who receives their rights and what gets taken away from us these days. The blockchain goes a long way towards eliminating this imbalance. No one needs a middleman on the blockchain. The blockchain isn't perfect, though. Some content should be censored, and not everything is suitable for public consumption.

However, rectifying this problem is as simple as creating rules on the network. Currently, there are no rules, just arbitrary judgments made on centralized networks. The blockchain also allows for ownership rights preservation thanks to smart contracts. These contracts can enforce complex criteria much better than any platform can.

Returning to the example of the film, you can store a record of ownership rights on the blockchain and enforce a smart contract with a counterparty. As long as the other person pays you a certain amount of Ethereum every month, they get to use the likeness of that media. If they violate terms by not paying you the precise amount, the contract automatically disables access.

Imagine a decentralized version of Youtube where access to the original content is gated like this. Instead of paying Youtube and Google money to merely host content, you can pay the creator directly. There won't be any need for middlemen like these platforms or even movie studios and other rent-seekers.

The biggest advantage is that rights are transferred fully back to the transacting parties. They aren't held hostage by a middleman in the name of compliance. Everything from intellectual property to property rights can be controlled by those who own them. As a result, the economy becomes more efficient.

The Seventh Principle

For an economy to prosper, every section of society has to be included within it. It's safe to say that the number of people not included in today's economy is far greater than the number of people who are. For instance, the elderly, the young, and those with poor credit aren't served by any banking institution. Instead, they're taken advantage of.

The situation is even worse in developing and underdeveloped countries, where rights are often ignored. Inclusion is perhaps the greatest principle of the blockchain. While the blockchain on which cryptocurrencies like Ethereum and Bitcoin rest are designed on TCP/IP protocols, they can be accessed without access to the internet.

That means you can access them with a simple flip phone. Services such as BitMoby, built on the Bitcoin network, allow people in underdeveloped countries to top up their mobile phone balance by sending the service an amount of Bitcoin. This service is great because there aren't any intermediaries that charge a fee or impose transaction limits.

The underserved portions of society typically cannot afford the bank account minimum balance. Everything is literally more expensive in our current society if you're poor. Your home is more expensive, your credit cards charge you more, and you cannot access benefits because your credit score is too low. Anyone can transact in cryptocurrencies because there are no limits imposed.

These days money is increasingly digitized, and cash has been marginalized. The result is that the underserved sections of society have been forced to move online and accept services that don't benefit them. They have to endure high minimum balances because they need a debit card to pay for goods.

In parts of Europe, businesses charge additional commissions for cash transactions which compounds the problem. The picture is even worse in less developed countries. When the economies of countries like Greece, Cyprus, and Turkey tanked, citizens were not allowed to withdraw large sums of money from their accounts. Some even froze the ability to withdraw cash.

Actions like these negatively impact the poorest sections of society. Without access to cash or credit, there's no way for these people to survive. Wealthier members of society will receive credit in such times and can get by, but this isn't an option for the underserved. A similar situation played out in 2016 in India when the government outlawed cash and embarked on a hairbrained exercise to replace the currency in circulation.

The result was a decimation of the agricultural sector and the closure of small businesses. Needless to say, any dissent over this move was quashed by the government on social media, with the platforms right alongside them. Blockchain-based networks make it impossible for such situations to occur. When Venezuela devalued its currency and banned foreign exchange, citizens traded Bitcoin for goods. It helped them beat hyperinflation and continue to live.

Aside from monetary benefits, there are social ones too. Centralized networks make it easy to squash dissent and propagate a single point of view. Decentralization allows dissent fully, and public debate has the opportunity to be more reasoned. There's no denying that a few extreme views will be circulated.

However, it isn't as if centralized networks prevent this from happening at the moment. The premise behind a centralized network lies in the incorruptibility of the entity in charge. Expecting Facebook and Twitter to be incorruptible is laughable, as these companies' actions have repeatedly shown.

Blockchain and decentralization are necessary for society to continue to advance and realize the original promise of the internet. It promises to end glass ceilings and dismantle the good old boys' clubs that currently rule centralized networks.

The bottom line is that these seven principles offer us a chance to redesign our economy along the lines of positive values. Centralization has served the world well this far, but thanks to the power they placed in the hands of central authorities, they've become corrupt. Individual rights no longer matter, and things like privacy and respect have become optional. Only those who can pay for it can access it.

Worse, centralized institutions gather our data but do not guarantee its safety. A single hack and your personal details are out there, ready for everyone to exploit. Even privacy-touting Apple has suffered from iCloud hacks that have exposed people's personal and most intimate details to the world. Apple has never paid the price for such lapses and continues to push people to store data on its cloud.

Even something as simple as browsing the web requires us to install privacy-related plugins to disable tracking. It ought to be the other way around. Our privacy should come pre-installed and not be an optional extra. Blockchain isn't just technological innovation; it offers us the chance to redesign our world. We'd be wise to take it as soon as possible.

4. Understanding Exchanges

Much like you need to use a platform to change money into different currencies, the same can be said for cryptocurrencies. Cryptocurrency exchanges normally facilitate exchanges between different cryptocurrencies as well as fiat currencies. The cryptocurrency exchanges tend to act as the middleman between both the buyer and the seller, and the exchanges to make money via commissions and other fees.

Centralized and Decentralized Exchanges

There are two different types of exchanges, and they have their fair share of differences. The most common and popular form of exchange is the **centralized exchange**, where the exchange official acts as a third party between the buyer and the seller. It is said that about 99% of all exchanges do occur via these platforms, and as a beginner, it is certainly recommended to start this way as well.

There are many advantages that come alongside this form of exchange. For example, the centralized platform is far more user-friendly, offering a familiar as well as a friendly way of trading in comparison to peer-to-peer transactions (decentralized exchanges), which can grow to be quite complex. Simplicity is certainly helpful in any format.

This platform is also far more reliable, adding an extra layer of security when one is actually trading. However, centralized exchanges are at a higher risk of hacking. There were many incidents where hacking has occurred, meaning extra work and effort has to be put in to trust the security of the platform software. Many exchanges hold the value of millions to even potentially billions of dollars worth of money, which makes it a huge digital target.

There are also a lot of transaction fees that come with working on centralized exchanges. The fees will depend on the exchange company you use. You also need to take into account how active you are as a trader, because the costs can add up pretty quickly.

Decentralized exchanges basically allow users to perform peer-to-peer transactions, where you are performing the exchanges directly with the people themselves rather than through a middleman.

When it comes to this platform, there is an automatically reduced risk of hacking, mainly because no one has the need to share third-party information, and because it does not have high-status in popularity, it is much less likely to be a target. These exchanges are automatically far safer in regards to cybercrime.

Market manipulation is a lot more difficult to build in a decentralized system. This is a massive advantage as it gives users a more even playing field. There is a lot of protection from both wash and fake trading.

One of the biggest advantages of crypto is the anonymous nature, so it is no surprise that having a decentralized exchange would play on the advantage of being anonymous as well. Therefore, you can use this platform with the knowledge that you will remain completely anonymous.

However, as mentioned before, decentralized exchanges are a very complex system, which means more time and effort needs to be spent on figuring the exchanges out. This can be very daunting for a beginner, and should only be used if you prefer the advantages of the decentralized system above the centralized system.

Cryptocurrency Exchanges to Consider

Binance

One of the largest cryptocurrency exchanges, in comparison to the trading volume, is Binance. Binance was published by a man named Changpen Zhao in 2017 in China. It has established a reputation of being one of the most reliable exchanges in the crypto trading world. Due to the hurdles faced in China, Binance is now being operated on the Malta islands in Europe. In September 2019, it also launched a platform specifically dedicated for the United States, called Binance US, which is compliant with the regulatory framework of the United States.

Binance is also one of the few exchanges that do not have fake trading volume or even wash trading activities. This means that it is a very transparent and open company. The more transparency that comes with a business, the better.

Binance has also focused on keeping itself up to date with the latest software and technology, making sure to keep up with the competition that is always rapidly advancing. It has managed to establish itself as one of the most popular gateways in the world of crypto.

Binance's History

Binance has attracted a lot of attention due to the cryptocurrency it trades, such as Ethereum and Bitcoin, as well as smaller tokens that are indeed micro-capped. Each token is needed to first fulfill all the requirements, as listed in the Binance rules before being run on this platform.

In 2019, Binance experienced a hack, where the thieves got away with $40 million in Bitcoin. However, the Binance SAFU (Secure Asset Fund Users) Fund had compensated for all the losses, and all the traders who suffered losses were reimbursed. This act certainly boosted Binance's popularity in the entirety of the crypto world.

SAFU is the emergency insurance that was implemented in 2018 as a way to protect trader's funds while they are using the exchange. Having your money insured adds a lot of extra security while you are using the exchange platform, which is especially ideal for a beginner.

Binance's Token

Even Binance has its own native token, called the Binance Coin or BNB, which adds a certain element of competition for its trading fee. The trading fee is reduced when using the platform's token, so fees are even cheaper if you consider using the Binance coin.

Opening a Binance Account

First, you will need to open an account by heading over to the Binance webpage, and you can start off by registering your email address and adding a password. Make sure again that the password you choose is long and complex, as you don't want to be hacked. Again, consider opening up two-factor authentication.

You will need to confirm your own personal details, as a verification of your identity will be required (as expected with a centralized project). This may take a while, as they are very focused on anti-laundering as well as avoiding criminal hubs (which in essence, boosts the security of using the platform, as you would want to make sure you are not dealing with criminals).

Then, after completing the verification process, you can add your funds using either a debit credit or bank accounts, depending on what exactly is supported in your country. Otherwise, you can consider purchasing Bitcoin or Ethereum somewhere else, such as Coinbase, and depositing them onto this platform. When you make the deposit, you can normally start trading within 20 minutes after the deposit has officially been confirmed.

Then you can finally start your journey of trading and investing. You can head to the "Exchange" button that is reflected on the top of the screen, and you can even choose if you want a basic or advanced chart/interface platform you to use. This all depends on what you are more comfortable with, assuming you have undergone paper trading and other training before jumping into live training.

eToro

eToro is a cheap and professional exchange used by some of the top traders in the world. It is an accessible trading platform that has cleverly devised a social element into investing. They were first launched in early 2006, and are now one of the world's largest communities in investment, with over 4.5 million users.

(geralt, 2018)

eToro has a unique feature called the 'copied trader,' where a person can sort through the variety of users and check out their trading history. This is especially handy if you are still learning how to trade and would like to see the choices others have made (do not copy-cat). Rather than having to ask the traders, you are free to view the decisions made and whether they were truly successful or not. If you do find someone whose trading choices seem to be doing well, you have the option to allocate funds that can automatically copy the trade. (This means the choices made with funding are in their hands rather than yours, and as the book pushes against it. So you know it is an option, but rather consider studying and learning from them as you build your own path.)

There is another program on eToro called the 'popular investor program.' It acts as a reward system for the number of copiers a specific person has (how many people copy your style and strategy of trading). This boosts the incentive to trade wisely, as people will only copy what they deem to be successful.

With the features tagged on eToro, you can consider this to be a great learning platform, and if you want to familiarize yourself with it without too much of a commitment, you can check it out on a demo account.

Again, before signing up, make sure you understand the basics of trading, and start small. It is never recommended to start investing large amounts of money as a beginner.

Opening an eToro Account

First, you will need to sign up at eToro.com; it is not an extensive application and is quite easy to set up. They do require your phone number in order to boost the security of your account.

It is recommended not to trade using CFD (Contract for Difference Trading) products, as most investors suffer a loss when deciding to do this. So keep this in mind as you start trading.

Next, you will want to fully complete your profile. This is when you input your basic personal information, basically verifying who you are, and have to answer a couple of trading questions. You don't have to be too concerned about the answers, but answer honestly.

Next, you will be directed to the place of deposit, where the minimum amount is normally $200.

Take your time browsing eToro, familiarizing yourself with this platform. You can start by creating a watchlist. This is creating lists of people whose trades you are interested in observing and perhaps considering copying if you want to.

Build your portfolio, which is the center of your journey. Here you can monitor the level of your performance, as well as watch your live trades unfold.

There is also a news feed you can watch, as this is the platform where people keep you updated on what they have been doing recently. This builds a closer community, as many people help each other along with their overall success.

Copy people are the very heart of the community. You can search through many of the traders you want to follow, or if you so, choose to copy.

Robinhood

This is not the legendary archer from the old tales, but rather, this Robinhood is another exchange platform for you to consider. Robinhood has been trending for quite some time, and many experts agree that it is likely to grow in popularity over time. As a crypto investor, you will be more interested in Robinhood Crypto, which acts as the exchange platform for cryptocurrency reviews.

The Robinhood Crypto app truly brought a new item to market in the mobile world. It made the promises for a far easier trading platform (again, ideal for beginners), and garnered the reputation of making trading life a lot simpler for everyone who decides to use it.

Robinhood Crypto supports many of the top cryptocurrencies, which allows you to trade in comfort and ease, and you can deposit or sell crypto to purchase the coins immediately. However, using other items, such as EFT (Electronic Funds Transfer) or stocks, may take up to 3 days to fulfill a trade.

Naturally, there has been a rise in concern about security itself on the crypto app. However, Robinhood did revert to using both online and offline wallets. As already said, offline wallets are far safer, thus boosting the overall security of using Robinhood. The majority of all the coins are kept in cold storage, and the company also carries insurance to make up for cybersecurity attacks and potential breaches.

However, Robinhood Crypto does have its fair share of limitations: one is the inability to withdraw your coins and the other is that you cannot transfer the cryptocurrencies elsewhere in your crypto wallet. However, Robinhood Crypto is working on correcting this limitation and upgrading itself to become more user-friendly.

The Cogworks of Robinhood

If you have a Robinhood account, it means you have instant access to the Robinhood Crypto account, and even instant access to buying crypto. If you don't, it may take some time to set everything up, including the verification process.

If you have sales from ETFs, it means the money you put in will take a little while longer to arrive, considering you are dealing with the middleman (your bank) and the middleman of the exchange (centralized). This is where patience is needed, but keep in mind you are signing up with Robinhood for its simplicity. If you are struggling to understand the heavy complexities of trading, then perhaps it is best to build your experience on the platform itself.

However, any proceeds that do come from crypto sales are immediately available for your use. And the moment you have the necessary funds, you can focus on buying the coins and start trading as soon as possible.

Selling the coins is as simplified as buying the coins on this app, and all you need to do is navigate the details page, insert the necessary information, and proceed with the sale itself. The moment the coins are sold, you can move on to your next venture with the funds you have received, making this a very effective and efficient trading platform, without the concern of having to wait days or weeks for money to arrive at your door after a trade.

Robinhood itself has taken measures to protect you from the volatile nature of the market, placing a collar on which you can either buy or sell at certain prices that fits within a specific range.

You also have the possibility to use a limit order, programming your account to buy or sell crypto once it reaches a certain price. This is a layer of protection, reducing the amount of loss you may receive when the market does not go in a good direction, but also picks up on opportunities that you may miss while you are away. It is an artificial intelligence that does the work of monitoring the trading activities 24/7 while you deal with other priorities.

Robinhood has gained most of its popularity through the design of the app itself. The app is very simple and easy, along with an appealing/aesthetic interface. It also happens to incorporate some of the latest technology, such as a biometric account where you can use your thumbprint to gain access or even your facial ID.

For the purchasing as well as selling of crypto, Robinhood is very easy and simple to use. Literally, with a couple of taps and swipes and clever strategizing (as a savvy investor should), you could easily complete a trade in a matter of minutes. And you can sell it at a rapid pace as well when need be. This certainly makes crypto more interesting for those who struggle to concentrate or figure out the inner workings of a trade. And again, this is quite ideal for a beginner who is still working on figuring everything out when it comes to cryptocurrency trading.

Robinhood also focuses on lower fees in comparison to the 'higher'-level trading sites. To help with people starting out and evening out the playing field, they have removed one of the biggest barriers that comes with trading on exchange platforms: the excessively high trading fees.

This means your sales and trades can work with smaller numbers without the trading fees eating up all your profits, so it is easier to start slow on this platform and still make a profit, regardless of the size of your trade (unless you go lower than the trading fee itself, which is not recommended).

However, there are a few drawbacks that come with trading on this app. One of them that had been mentioned before, is it's functionality. Withdrawal is normally quite an issue, and although you are able to withdraw to your bank account, this does mean incorporating the traditional capital tax that comes alongside it (making the withdrawal of your crypto quite expensive).

There is also a concerning lack of transparency that comes with these prices. Some 'fees' that are supposedly free are just tacked on with the prices people deem the cryptocurrency to be, and this is where Robinhood is actually making the money.

And the team of Robinhood itself has made no comments on the settings of the price of the app, which again, in and of itself can be quite a concerning matter. Transparency is always a big recommendation when it comes to businesses: the less transparency, the more issues the company itself may be trying to hide.

There are also a couple of security concerns, although, unlike some other exchanges, there have been no reports of any large-scale hacks. However, there has been a fair share of cases of isolated hacking occurring in accounts. So the security that is offered on the app is not altogether riskier nor altogether safer than what is being offered on other exchanges. You will have to keep this in mind if safety is a huge priority for you.

So after seeing a little more about Robinhood, you may be wondering whether it is really the right app for you. Each exchange certainly brings something a little different to the table, and it is up to you to decide which exchange suits you the best.

Other Top Exchanges to Consider

Now, having looked in-depth at some of the top exchanges you can consider as a beginner, here is a peek at some of the other top exchanges you can use.

Coinbase

Coinbase and Coinbase Pro have proven to have simplified and easy forms of transactions. The software itself is very transparent, with strong security latched onto it. It is also a very popular form of exchange, and as you work with cryptocurrency and trading you will most likely hear about Coinbase.

Coinbase has a solid variety of altcoins you can trade with. It is also quite user-friendly, and the level of liquidity tacked onto it is high.

But keep in mind, the prices are higher if you are not using Coinbase Pro (trading fees), and a person does not have actual control over their wallet keys. This means that you may need to have another wallet outside of the exchange to store the majority of your coins to make sure they are fully secure.

Coinbase also has a lot of issues with fraudulent coins as well as exchanges that have been quite shady. This means many people avoid these exchanges due to security and higher chances of getting caught in a scam. But Coinbase has offered wallets that are insured for investors as well as insurance for any data breaches that may occur. If you are more advanced, you may consider getting Coinbase Pro, which is more complex, but has a far greater variety of options when it comes to both charts and indicators. This is if you want to trade at a higher level, and would like to have the tools to deal with that.

Cash App

Cash app is another user-friendly exchange app you can use that has quite a few flexible options available, such as the use of other crypto wallets and withdrawals. It is a peer-to-peer money transfer that can work like Venmo or even Zelle. You also have the ability to withdraw Bitcoin itself if you want, and again, being user-friendly makes the life of a trader a lot easier, as there are many fewer frustrations and issues you would have to face.

However, it only actually supports the use of Bitcoin and not any other crypto. There is also a 3% charge when you are sending money through your credit card, and you have a set number of days as well weekly withdrawal limits.

Cash App allows users to invest in other stocks, Bitcoin, or EFTs in a way that Robinhood can as well. It has a simplified mobile interface, making it ideal for people who are investing for the very first time, and beginners who are very much interested in buying Bitcoin.

Having the ability to withdraw your crypto from an exchange is important in the crypto community. With Robinhood, although you can both invest and trade in your cryptocurrencies, you cannot actually withdraw the crypto and spend it in any way you desire. With the Cash App you are fully capable of doing so, but you are actually still unable to gain control of your private keys, which is always a security issue, as you may struggle to prove or gain ownership of the coin if you are not careful.

BiSQ

This is by far one of the best-decentralized forms of exchanges out there. BiSQ is an open-source software that does not have any KYC (Know Your Customer) requirements and is available if you are interested in dabbling in decentralized exchanges in the near future. There are more than 25 varied options you have to pay for, and you can also use it on a mobile app both for Android and also for iOS.

However, the transaction speeds are known to be quite slow, and considering the lack of popularity in using trading volumes, that can be quite slow as well. It is not exactly designed for active forms of trading either.

Following the premise that Bitcoin has set down, there is no requirement for you to legally provide any identification, location, or even nationality on BiSQ. For someone who likes to stay anonymous, this is certainly one of the largest benefits. Considering that many people use crypto for the exact same reason, why not use an exchange that has the same goals?

There are many who argue against the possibility of giving opportunities to criminal activities. There is a flip-side, where people can open accounts that have less-developed banking systems. All you really need is an internet connection. There are millions of people around the world that have minimal access to a bank, which means at the end of the day it inhibits them from trading if they want to. BiSQ very much provides them this opportunity, as it is a good solution for the most part.

It is a downloadable form of software. There is no central point that can fail or be taken down. There is no main point of authority, which means no one ever has any control over the funds of the user, which is vastly different from centralized exchanges. For example, Coinbase, a centralized exchange has every right to seize the funds you have if they deem your activities to be suspicious, regardless of whether what you are doing is actually legal in your specific location.

BISQ is also instantly accessible for anyone who has access to the internet and has a computer or a smartphone. This certainly makes it ideal for anyone who wants to have privacy.

A person has to take into account the lower trading volumes and slower transactions, but for some people, the benefits far outweigh the drawbacks. And again, it is up to you to decide.

When you are looking for a cryptocurrency trading or investing platform, it is best to choose the exchange that suits your goals. Whether it may be cheaper fees, easier design, or even a variety of coins, these are all matters you will have to consider when approaching the exchange. So it is best to have your goals in place first before deciding on the exchange, rather than adapting to the exchange. After all, this is your journey, and you best make sure you are actually comfortable with the steps you are taking.

5. What Is a Non-Fungible Token?

A Non-Fungible Token, or NFT, is a cryptographic token that allows a digital product to have an identity that is unique or authentic and a good and true product that can be traced. It allows monitoring of who has it and how much it costs, to be able to assign a value to it in a given market.

NFTs are advanced resources checked by blockchain innovation that can represent anything from computerized fine arts to ball features to energized GIFs. Regardless of whether the NFT is unique or only one of a group, the utilization of Blockchain to "mint" everything gives evidence of its realness and who made and possesses it.

A Non-Fungible Token is a cryptographic symbol that can be extraordinary and unrepeatable. However, one that can't be partitioned can be utilized to represent objects in the real or advanced world, confirm their attributes and their owner, while maintaining the entirety of this inside a portrayal on a blockchain through an agreement.

A genuine illustration of an NFT would be a collectible. A computerized card of a well-known game figure with a restricted presence and extraordinarily advanced markings is an ideal illustration of an advanced NFT. Be that as it may, the equivalent occurs if, for instance, the cards are genuine, and we carry their properties to the computerized world utilizing a blockchain. For this situation, the actual card has an advanced portrayal, yet said portrayal would just serve to control the ownership of the actual card, permitting us consistently to follow its realness, track its history of ownership, and confirm that it is, without doubt, the card we need.

What Makes NFTs So Exceptional?

Unlike what occurs with cryptographic forms of money, NFTs can't be traded with one another since no two NFTs are interchangeable. Your letter from a Crypto Kitty is exceptional, providing value only for a single item, which cannot be compared to any other.

A large portion of these "tokens" (which can be coins, stamps, masterpieces, or crypto felines, for instance) depend on the agreed standards of the Ethereum organization and its Blockchain.

This has made it simple to work with them when purchasing and selling them. Administrations like MetaMask or MyEtherWallet (wallets that permit communication with Ethereum) are benchmarks in this kind of exchange. What's more, NFTs have a few useful qualities:

- **Unusually extraordinary: these resources have numerous analogies with masterpieces of which there might be duplicates (it is much simpler to make duplicates of advanced works), yet here the proprietor can affirm that they are the**

sole and real proprietor of the first work, even though it tends to be effortlessly shared on the Internet. It's an interesting circumstance and an innovation in the way we view craftsmanship's physical and computerized works.

- ***Non-Interoperable:*** *a CryptoPunk can't be utilized as a character in the CryptoKitties game or the other way around. The same goes for collectibles like exchanging cards as well. A Blockchain Heroes card can't be played in the Gods Unchained exchanging game.*
- ***Resolute:*** *NFTs can't be partitioned into smaller sections like bitcoin satoshis. They exist solely as a complete unit. This contrasts with digital forms of money. They have an agreed worth as a single item or token without division. You can't have 1/1000 of a Crypto Kitty.*
- ***Indestructible:*** *because all NFT information is stored on the Blockchain through agreements, no token can be eradicated, removed, or reproduced.*
- ***Irrefutable:*** *an extra benefit of recording official ownership information on the Blockchain is that things (for example, advanced craftsmanship) can be followed back to the first maker, which permits pieces to be confirmed without the requirement for external checking. The Blockchain makes it conceivable to check something that is considerably more intricate to show or confirm with points like craftsmanship gathering or stamps. For instance, the Blockchain keeps a record including who has purchased or sold an NFT and who is its current (supreme) owner, as well as the original maker from whom that advanced resource was bought.*
- **Outright possession:** transfer of ownership for tokens is permanent, which means gamers and authorities retain control of their purchased NFTs, not the organizations that make them. This contrasts with purchasing things like music from the iTunes store, where customers don't claim ownership of what they're purchasing—they buy the permit to tune in to the music. The information about an NFT that is stored in the Blockchain through an agreement (Smart Contract) makes it difficult to eradicate, erase or recreate.

How Are Non-Fungible Tokens Utilized?

Non-Fungible Tokens are utilized to confirm an obvious computerized defect and advanced possession and the chance of resource collaborations across various stages. NFTs are utilized in a few explicit applications requiring one-of-a-kind advanced components, like cryptography (uncommon craftsmanship), cryptographic collectibles, and cryptographic games.

Crypto exchanging games are the most recent utilization of game-related NFTs. Companies, for example, Age of Chains and Rare Pepes, utilized the Counterparty convention to give Bitcoin-based Blockchain exchanging cards as NFTs in 2016.

Craftsmanship was one of the principal employments of the Blockchain CryptoPunks Launch in 2017 June. This paved the way for the specialty of encryption in the Ethereum 6 blockchain. DADA.art was produced from the CryptoPunks model and, in October 2017, it opened the principal market for cryptographic artistry.

Afterward, famous blockchain games, like CryptoKitties, utilized indispensable chips in the Ethereum blockchain. NFTs are utilized to represent game resources and are overseen by the client, not the game engineer. This permits the property to be exchanged in outsider business sectors without the authorization of the game designer. The cryptographic expressions are Nifty Gateway, Rarible, Super Rare, Famous Origins, and MakersPlace.

NFTs can represent sales of advanced works like computerized craftsmanship, computer game components, and music documents. There are different structures for the creation and issuance of NFTs. The most noteworthy of these is ERC-721, a standard for the issuance and exchanging of non-fungible resources on the Ethereum blockchain.

A later improved standard is ERC-1155. It empowers a solitary agreement to contain both Fungible and Non-Fungible Tokens, opening an entirely different scope of potential outcomes. The normalization of the issuance of NFTs permits a more serious level of interoperability, which at last advantages the customer. This means that exceptional resources can be moved between various applications effortlessly. Perhaps you are hoping to store and look upon the excellence of your NFTs; you can do that in Trust Wallet. Like other blockchain tokens, your NFT will exist in a location.

NFTs can be exchanged in open commercial centers, like OpenSea. These business sectors connect purchasers with merchants, and the estimation of every token is novel. Normally, NFTs are inclined to value changes because of fluctuating market interest.

The activity of NFTs can shift contingent upon the blockchain stage where they are executed. Each blockchain stage has a progression of capacities that make NFTs ready to act somehow. Consequently, for instance, the NFTs in Ethereum may have contrasting inactivity (inside) in comparison with those of TRON or EOS.

Nonetheless, these distinctions are related to changes that are made, so the activity of agreements adjusts to the blockchain framework where they are executed—for example, the programming language utilized, how access is taken care of, and the cutoff points and assets that can be utilized inside the organization. Of the rest, the activity of the NFTs follows certain boundaries that we can call standard and, which by and large, follow the construction directed by Ethereum with its ERC-721 and the latest ERC-1155 standards.

With the making of ERC-721 and ERC-1155, Ethereum figured out how to utilize several apparatuses that enormously encouraged NFT stages inside Ethereum. To do this, it furnished both standard savvy contracts with a progression of capacities and abilities that all NFTs may require for their control and advancement. Subsequently, for instance, the ERC-721 and ERC-1155 permit you to make, move, change and even obliterate NFTs.

When you buy an NFT, you buy a token and a piece of art linked to that token. The sold art can be a unique piece or edition of a work, but each token is unique and unrepeatable. Another very important feature of NFTs is the fact that they are indivisible. This means that you cannot send a part of a Non-Fungible Token to someone (unlike Bitcoin).

The purchase-sale transaction is made in cryptocurrencies and registered in the Blockchain, which allows a permanent record of that purchase and provides proof of ownership.

What Changes With Ethereum 2.0 (Scalability And Security)

Ethereum today / Ethereum 2.0 - A game-changer / It's effect on Miners

Sweet joy and happiness are what I feel anytime I get to talk about certain altcoins such as this particular one for instance. Knowing fully well that it is an altcoin that is really moving fast and found its way up the ladder to be in a serious competitive position, I love it. What can I say about this beauty that will be enough for you to consent to the investment of cryptocurrencies?

How about a little bit of revision? Ethereum is a cryptocurrency (altcoin) that has got more attention as being one of the decentralized networks and with a platform that supported different forms of Smart Contracts that got more attention during the pandemic, and a lot of people used these Smart Contracts to gather lots of this cryptocurrency. Forsage, Million Money and Lion Share just to mention a few, are parts of Smart Contracts built on the blockchain of the cryptocurrency Ethereum, since it has a network that was created and operating without any interference or control from any outsider and it is well secured against any fraudulent activity.

Ethereum is the second cryptocurrency after Bitcoin (BTC). And, it has a very large market capitalization. Pretty early this month the other version of the cryptocurrency that we have been waiting for, that is the upgraded version (Ethereum 2.0) of Ethereum came to reality. There is an update already from the founder of the cryptocurrency, Vitalik Buterin.

You should not forget the crucial role that this cryptocurrency played, since it served more as a roadblock remover talking about Smart Contracts and it has set a fortified ground for any or many developers to make use of its platform.

Ethereum (ETH) is Ethereum 1.0, do not forget that I said that it uses proof-of-work consensus to complete all requirements or the work to be done. At least we all know that that is the first and initial algorithm of the cryptocurrency's blockchain network. The summary of it is that there have to be some certain participants of the blockchain.

Now that the use-to-be consensus has been modified and it is now proof-of-stake, this is a symbol or a sign of something big enough to change the game. Proof-of-stake runs as some participants also referred to as validators, protect the whole betting on which of the block is going to be valid next, and whoever gets the right bet will be rewarded while, those that do not get the right one, are penalized for it.

Proof-of-stake happens to be more energy efficient because it does not require making use of great computation in order to unravel the whole puzzle. Ethereum (ETH) 2.0, with its new consensus, is to arrive with so many attractiveness, as it has a more fortified or heightened security level and with its ability to change in scale or size.

It is highly projected that, with this newly modified consensus, more energy will be saved. But the thing is, miners are also the participants and validators of transactions like crypto-staking, and they have been given the responsibility of examining both transactions and the sum of money and the actual length of time any holder could hold their assets for, which is to give them a meaningful and secured position from what seems difficult to be dislodged and an uncomely merit in the market with that much power and awareness capable enough to give a tacit suggestion into the concentrated or centralized system.

There is an argument going on that staking will not do anything good than causing a centralized effect on the network despite the issue that led to the saying that concerning proof-of-work (PoW) “the larger the mining farm, the higher the return due to economies of scale.”

Opposite of what had earlier been expected, with proof-of-stake (PoS), little economies of scale are present in this consensus such that, cost of staking is to be so much similar either a person is to stake for instance 40 Ethereum (ETH) or 40,000 Ethereum (ETH).

Furthermore, the recent projection for my beauty, Ethereum (ETH) 2.0, the public network should accept between 1,000 and 5,000 TPS, and you just cannot try to make any comparison of this cryptocurrency (Ethereum 2.0) modified consensus with Ethereum (ETH) 1.0 as it can at least allow 30 TPS.

Going through many people's thoughts on this there is one I love and cannot just wave it away. Zipmex says “it will take several years as it is highly likely that by that point, people will have already been using layer 2 solution such as rollups to address scalability issues.”

There is a high increment in the consciousness and the ongoing large number of adoptions everywhere. Some of us believe that the price is actually being pushed by the notion. But taking a critical look at things, the sum of transactions and the daily gas are fixed in the green with the network usage of over 90%.

Ethereum has a feature for protecting exchange details and assets, you just have to be updated with the news of the cryptocurrency Ethereum (ETH), as concerned with its movement and its directed change. It is always imperative and resourceful having a framework that projects into the future as the time is still very far.

2020 has made many activities or processes move online because of the pandemic that gave rise to staying at home and social distancing. It really hastened every form of activities that are or were frequently happening that have been digitalized to grow and develop faster including the speed of payment to become even faster and easier.

The pandemic legacy was not just death or recession, it opened the eyes of people to new opportunities. This inconvenience we faced triggered the urge we had, and many of us moved our businesses online. The same way it contributed to the advancement of the blockchain and many Smart Contracts and it gained the advancement as a result of not just the most obvious reason, which is the pandemic, but because of its decentralized nature of the network of the cryptocurrency Ethereum (ETH), and it gave rise to its prominence.

The construction of a plan of action regarding Ethereum 2.0 has actually given many goosebumps already. This is the future of a blockchain community. We will definitely have many surprise packages as regards the advanced cryptocurrency, Ethereum (ETH) 2.0.

I am not a guru—in fact, I put a lot of hard work into things before I can be able to say “I have got this.” Neither am I some seer, but I really do think that the steady rate of Ethereum over the past few weeks is not some miracle of God, but because of the promising values of the cryptocurrency in the offing which is Ethereum (ETH) 2.0 that has shifted from its used-to-be proof-of-work (PoW) to proof-of-stake (PoS) consensus.

No one should take away the leading from the jungle or stop it from roaring, neither can we say that the lioness being the hunter to keep quiet or stop hunting. Bitcoin (BTC) has the highest market capitalization and value, but for an altcoin, Ethereum has done and is doing pretty well.

As an altcoin, this cryptocurrency might just be the most essentially planned endeavor, with an actual goal and accomplishment in several steps or stages in the blockchain virtual world. Unarguably, the cryptocurrency (ETH) Ethereum has the second largest market capitalization in all the cryptocurrencies that we have and it is second to Bitcoin (BTC) and it is like a vessel carrying other vessels that are smaller.

What I am saying is that Ethereum allows some other blockchain projects and applications such as Defi applications to advance. The cryptocurrency is stretching its hands wide and ready to show us its second generation and how much more it has gotten to the point of growth and development or advancement in everything its first generation has been offering to us.

What has been a concern about Ethereum (ETH) 2.0 is that, as much as it likes carrying smaller vessels on with its blockchain, the more applications get higher and higher on this blockchain, the costs get increased and there is a depletion in the level of its speed.

I remember using the abbreviation of TPS earlier, I am sorry I did not break that down. Transactions per second, that is the meaning of that abbreviation. And, whenever there is a congestion in the cryptocurrencies (ETH 1.0), the transaction per second has reached its limit already and there be a serious hindrance to any Ethereum (ETH) 1.0 applications' designing or programming.

When it comes to the vision behind the conception of the cryptocurrency Ethereum (ETH) 2.0, it is going to be a need to groom Ethereum (ETH) until it becomes fully capable or mature enough to take up the responsibility of assisting humanity.

In the grooming stage, as it is still in, there is an essential need to make so many sensible and creative modifications to be the advancement of its characteristics such as security, ability to be sustainable, and its size. For Ethereum (ETH) to be fully exploited, it needed to shift its consensus algorithm from proof-of-work (PoW) to proof-of-stake (PoS).

The plan is not even using electronic machines (computers) as nodes to a miner, it is basically the users, staking their Ethereum (ETH) to be a validator and given the kind of responsibilities the miners in the consensus algorithm of proof-of-work (PoW).

Miners too stake but, they are to stake 32 Ethereum (ETH) to actually become a validator. We are expecting energy efficiency on a very great level at least better than before, barriers to entry reduction, hardware required becoming way reduced and to buttress everything, better or higher immunity to any form or sign of centralization.

Ethereum (ETH) 2.0 is designed to increase its previous shard chains, which is intended to cause a significant advancement in the speed of its transaction per second (TPS).

Sharding is the kind of a careful step-by-step procedure taken with the intention of splitting a database horizontally enough to give a spreading impact on the load, as it is viewed to reduce the Ethereum's (ETH) network congestion and finally, increasing the transaction per second (TPS) by creating new chains.

There is another chain involved in this matter of Ethereum (ETH) 2.0; that chain is referred to as "Beacon Chain" and is known as a "Phase 0" on the Ethereum's complex roadmaps, it is a fundamental part of Ethereum (ETH) 2.0.

The intended plan is for it to be a forerunner for proof-of-stake (Pos) to the Ethereum (ETH) system, and to take the role of a coordinator. This particular chain received state details from Shard Chains (64 shard chains) and ensuring its availability for other Shard Chains in the system just to ensure the complete synchronicity in the network. It also has an added responsibility of managing validators, from stake registration to issuing rewards and penalties too.

The validators happen to be the main participants of Ethereum (ETH) 2.0 and are charged with the responsibility of keeping the network protected throughout the year and seven days a week.

The higher percentage of the whole digital programming for keeping the Ethereum (ETH) 2.0 network always online and so active pertains to the validators, and their major and biggest responsibility have is simply to guarantee their individual internet connection is not fluctuating and all the machines they are in charge of are all very connected to a stable source of electrical power.

Differences Between Cryptocurrencies and Token

A Non-Fungible Token (NFT) is a blockchain-based cryptographic token that denotes a single asset. These can be entirely digital assets or tokenized copies of physical assets. Since NFTs aren't identical, they may serve as evidence of legitimacy and possession in the digital world. Each unit of an asset is similar and virtually indistinguishable from one another, which is referred to as fungibility. Fiat currencies, for instance, are fungible so that individual units can be exchanged for any other equal unit. A hundred-dollar bill may be substituted for any different actual hundred-dollar bill. This is critical for an asset that is intended to be used as a means of exchange.

Fungibility is an essential feature for currencies since it allows for free trade, and there is no way to determine the past of each particular unit potentially. Nevertheless, for collectible pieces, this isn't a good quality to have. What if we might add a unique identifier to an individual unit rather than creating Bitcoin-like digital assets? As a result, each of them will be distinct from the others (i.e., non-fungible). This is basically what an NFT is.

What You Should Know

NFTs are one-of-a-kind cryptographic tokens that can't be duplicated on a blockchain. Real-world objects such as artwork, music, IDs, events, and real-estate can be represented using NFTs. Such real-world, actual assets can be "tokenized" to make them more profitable to buy, sell, and exchange while also lowering the chances of theft. NFTs may also reflect people's authenticity, copyrights, and other things.

Collectibles, like digital paintings, sports tickets, and copyright, account for a large portion of the current demand for NFTs. NBA Top Shot, a space to acquire Non-Fungible tokenized NBA experiences in the form of digital cards, is probably the most lauded place. A few of such cards have fetched vast amounts of money in auctions. Jack Dorsey, the CEO of Twitter, recently announced a link to a tokenized copy of his first tweet, in which he wrote, “just setting up my Twitter.” The auction for the NFT edition of the very first tweet has already reached $2.5 million.

Understanding NFTs

Cryptocurrencies, similar to physical currency, are fungible, meaning they can be substituted or swapped for one another. A Bitcoin in the UK, for instance, is still worth the same as another Bitcoin in the US. A single unit of Ether is often equivalent to the same unit of Ether anywhere in the world. Cryptocurrencies are ideal for use as a stable means of exchange in the digital world because of their fungibility.

NFTs, like Cryptocurrencies, have ownership information that makes it simple to identify and pass tokens among owners. In NFTs, holders may also add metadata or features related to the asset. Fair exchange tokens, for instance, can be used to depict coffee beans. Artists may also mark their digital work in the metadata with their personal signature.

Cryptokitties is probably the most well-known application of NFTs. Cryptokitties, which were first introduced in November 2017, are digital versions of cats with unique identifiers on the Ethereum blockchain. Every kitty is one-of-a-kind and has a monetary value in ether. They multiply amongst themselves, producing new youngsters with specific features and values than their parents. In the space of few weeks of their introduction, crypto kitties had amassed a fan base that had invested over $20 million in the ether on buying, feeding, and caring for them. Some devotees invested over $100,000 on the project.

Although the first use case for crypto kitties may seem insignificant, subsequent ones have much more significant business consequences. For instance, NFTs have been used in private equity and real estate investments. The capacity to supply escrow for various forms of NFTs, from events tickets to copyright, into a single financial transaction is one of the consequences of allowing several forms of tokens in a contract.

Importance of Non-Fungible Tokens

Business quality is perhaps the most apparent advantage of NFTs. Converting a tangible asset to a virtual asset simplifies procedures and eliminates mediators. On a blockchain, NFTs reflect virtual or physical artwork, removing the need for representatives and allowing artists to interact directly with their fan base. They can also help businesses develop their processes. An NFT for a beer bottle, for instance, would make it easier for various players in the supply chain to communicate with it and monitor its authenticity, development, and selling during the process. Ernst & Young, a consulting company, has already created a similar solution for one of its customers.

Non-fungible tokens are equally great for managing identities. Look at the case of physical passports, which must be shown at any point of entry and exit. It is possible to simplify the entry and exit systems for countries by transforming each passport into NFTs, each with its own special identifying features. NFTs may also be used for identity management in the digital world, expanding on this use case.

The emergence of new opportunities and forms of investment is the most promising possibility for NFTs. Imagine a tract of land that has been divided into several parts, each with its own set of features and property types. One division might be located near a beach, while another is a shopping center, and another is a residential neighborhood. Each piece of land is special, valued separately, and depicted by an NFT based on its features. By integrating necessary metadata into each specific NFT, real estate trading can be streamlined, which is a complicated and cumbersome process.

6. Investing in DeFi

You may be wondering why DeFi is so appealing as an investment. To understand what makes DeFi so appealing, you need to have a comprehensive understanding of Ethereum.

Ethereum is a decentralized blockchain platform that runs smart contracts and applications. The platform can be used to create digital assets such as tokens, cryptocurrencies, and more. These digital assets are then traded in decentralized exchanges such as the popular Binance exchange or Coinbase Pro exchange.

The ability for anyone to create their own token or cryptocurrency opens up a new world of opportunities for developers who want to create their own blockchain-based projects without being limited by the traditional financial institutions.

Differences between DeFi and Ethereum

DeFi is a decentralized blockchain financial system that is made up of smart contracts. Ethereum is a blockchain-based platform for which developers can build decentralized applications or 'DApps'.

DApps are decentralized applications that run on blockchain technology. The idea behind DApps is to cut out the middleman and allow for direct transactions between two parties. This could be beneficial for ride-sharing services, for example, because it would allow for more transparency and save people money in the long run.

Ethereum has been around for almost 10 years now and it has proven to be quite versatile in the sense that it can be used for many different purposes. However, Ethereum's focus on smart-contract capabilities has led to it being largely dominated by DApps.

DeFi and Ethereum differ in many aspects, but they both are built on top of blockchain technology and focus on decentralization.

The main difference between DeFi and Ethereum is that while DeFi focuses on the financial aspect of things. Ethereum is more focused on building DApps. DeFi's smart contracts are different from Ethereum's in that they can be customized by users to suit their needs and create new financial instruments.

In addition, DeFi uses off-chain transactions while Ethereum uses on-chain transactions. Off-chain transactions are faster and cheaper than on-chain transactions. DeFi can be used for payments and exchanges without having to wait for the confirmation of an Ethereum transaction.

Growth of the DeFi Industry

The DeFi industry is relatively new, and it has experienced exponential growth. The DeFi market grew from $700 million in 2018 to $13 billion in 2020. This rapid growth can be attributed to a number of factors, including the rise of cryptocurrency and blockchain technology.

Digital currencies and decentralized platforms have gained a lot of popularity in recent years. They are also becoming a popular investment option. Growth in the DeFi market reflects the potential of digital currencies and decentralized platforms to offer a new form of investment. The DeFi market allows people to trade digital assets and borrow funds from other people or from the blockchain itself.

According to data provided by Statista, as of January 12, 2022, the value of cryptocurrency held in DeFi worldwide is $80,780.6 million, and this amount continues to grow steadily. Even though the growth has not been completely linear and has faced different obstacles such as the increase in "gas prices" (which are the transaction fees of Ethereum) over the past year. But even so, the trend has always been one of continuous growth.

The digital economy is also creating a foundation for digital financial services that can be offered without any restrictions on who can use them or where they can be delivered. The goal of DeFi is to build a foundation for permissionless networks and the development of blockchain-based financial products for an emerging digital economy.

Is It Worth Investing in DeFi in 2022?

Despite the fact that the crypto market is still bearish, DeFi is still worth investing in. We are witnessing only the beginning. The most important thing to consider when investing in crypto assets, or in any asset for that matter, is what kind of return on investment (ROI) you are going to get.

You also need to consider your outlook. If you want to hold your crypto investment for the long term, can you weather its volatility? Ask yourself what you would do if the market turns bearish and your asset loses value over a few months or years.

Primary things to consider before diving into the world of DeFi include:

- *What are your goals?*
- *How much time do you have available to invest in DeFi and track your holdings?*
- How much risk are you willing to take?

There are also many other factors a new user should consider to determine if they are ready to deal with DeFi.

One of the most important considerations is the level of security. If you want to invest in a cryptocurrency, you will want a high level of security.

Ask yourself if you will be using crypto coins for daily purchases. Are you comfortable with using cryptocurrencies for your daily purchases and payments? If you do not want to deal with daily or even hourly crypto volatility, it may not be worth it for your business or personal use case.

Ways to Invest in DeFi

DeFi Assets

In the past, investing in crypto assets was not easy. You needed to put in a huge amount of time and resources to research the right project and make sure you were investing in a good one.

However, with the rise of DeFi, investing in crypto assets is becoming easier. DeFi provides investors with a way to invest without worrying about whether they are investing into the right project or not and without the need to track their investments in great detail.

The best way to invest in DeFi is through trading DeFi tokens. These tokens represent the value of different networks, applications, and technologies that are built on top of blockchain technology. Some of the most popular assets are MakerDAO's Dai, 0x, and OmiseGO. However, there are other assets available such as Aragon Network and Augur's REP. These DeFi assets are often traded on exchanges like Binance or KuCoin.

The ultimate goal of DeFi assets is to provide a secure and liquid investment option for individuals who want to invest in DeFi networks, applications, or protocols. They are used to represent ownership of a project's network or protocol and to pay for services within the network or protocol.

DeFi assets are meant to make it easier for investors to invest in DeFi projects through the use of a digital asset and make it easier for users to purchase these assets with various cryptocurrencies like Bitcoin, Ether, and others.

DeFi Staking

DeFi staking means investing in tokens that represent DeFi networks, applications or protocols, which can be traded on exchanges for profit. Basically, it is a method of investing in decentralized networks and applications through tokens or crypto assets that represent these networks or protocols. The more you stake, the more you get paid, as long as you're holding your tokens in your wallet.

Staking is the process of locking up your tokens so that they cannot be used for trading or sold. If you have some Ether, Bitcoin, or any other cryptocurrency, you can use it as a staking tool and earn passive income from it.

This method can be used by investors to earn passive income without having to manage any of the underlying assets themselves.

DeFi Yield Farming

The market for DeFi assets is currently dominated by crypto exchanges. The most popular exchange, Binance, has a volume of $76 billion per day and the second largest, KuCoin, has a volume of $385 million per day.

DeFi yield farming is an innovative way to get involved in the current market for DeFi assets. It allows you to invest in a pool of DeFi assets that are traded on these two exchanges without having to buy them yourself and without creating any risk for you as an investor. It's a new approach in the world of cryptocurrency investment.

The main idea behind yield farming is to invest in a token that has a potential for appreciation but which also has a high yield. The yield is usually calculated as the ratio between current price and future price—the higher the yield, the more you will gain when you sell your tokens at their higher future price.

Yield farming is similar to traditional loans that we know are made through banks, when the loan is repaid with interest. With yield farming, the concept is the same: cryptocurrency accumulated in an account can be invested in different types of DeFi assets that can generate more income than they would generate if they were just sitting idle.

It allows you to invest in DeFi networks and earn passive income from their growth. Yield farming is not new to the investment world but it has only recently been introduced to the crypto market.

Yield farming provides a way to diversify your portfolio.

DeFi Lending

As stated before, DeFi is a type of lending platform for cryptocurrencies. DeFi lending platforms enable users to lend their crypto to someone else and earn interest on it. Some DeFi lending platforms allow users to trade DeFi assets—tokens used to represent DeFi networks, apps, or protocols—while others are simply used for lending and borrowing crypto coins like banks would lend money.

In general, this sort of transaction allows users to borrow fiat currency credit at lower rates than the traditional cryptocurrency exchange market. The platform also makes it easier for users to access a range of loans for both personal and business uses. The benefit to long-term investors is the option of lending assets and passively earning interest.

DeFi Funds

There are a lot of DeFi funds and trusts you can invest in if you're looking for a more passive way to invest in the ecosystem. You will have to do your research on which trust or fund is right for you. What is important is to make sure that the fund or trust has a strong team behind it and a good performance history.

With that said, the DeFi space offers many different types of funds, trusts, and other investments. There are three types of funds that can be found on the DeFi market: hedge funds, venture capital funds, and private equity funds. Venture capital and private equity funds are usually closed to new investors while hedge funds are open to new investors.

Hedge funds in crypto are a new and exciting field that has been gaining popularity over the past few years. These funds offer many different opportunities for investors who want to profit from cryptocurrency. The main focus of a traditional hedge fund is to make money by investing client money in various assets, such as stocks or bonds. This concept easily translates to the DeFi environment.

Hedge funds can also invest in cryptocurrency, but they invest much more conservatively than other investment vehicles.

With the introduction of crypto hedge funds, investors can diversify their portfolios and avoid investing in the same companies again and again. The idea behind these crypto hedge funds is to leverage the volatility of cryptocurrencies to make profits for investors. They offer a high-risk/high-reward strategy for those looking for a quick buck.

Venture capital funds are new to DeFi. A venture capital fund is an investment company that provides capital to startups or small businesses with high growth potential. It is typically funded by institutional investors such as private equity firms, family offices, and hedge funds. Venture capital funds can also be funded by individuals who invest their personal savings or retirement accounts.

In the DeFi space, a venture capital fund can invest in decentralized protocols and blockchain projects and use cryptocurrency as the main asset. They provide investors with a way to participate in the growth of this emerging sector. The main focus of these funds is to provide funding for blockchain projects that have no other way of securing financing.

These funds are an alternative to traditional venture capital firms which invest in startups. The startups are usually funded by venture capital firms and then sold off when they become successful.

Private equity funds invest in companies through stock purchases. Private equity funds have been around for decades, and they have been a key part of the economy since the Industrial Revolution.

Private equity funds are transforming into decentralized financial instruments and blockchain-based investments. Blockchain is changing the way private equity funds operate. The fund managers can now invest their capital using blockchain technology and digital assets, which also offers more liquidity to investors than traditional private equity funds.

Private equity crypto funds are now a popular investment option for people looking to get into the crypto market. The money raised from these funds is then used to invest in cryptocurrencies and blockchain startups.

Private equity crypto funds are launching with the hope that they can help make the world of cryptocurrency a more accessible one. They want to make it easier for people to invest in cryptocurrencies, which will ultimately lead to more mainstream adoption.

One of the first private equity crypto funds was launched by Block Tower Capital back in 2017. Since then, over 620 crypto funds have been launched worldwide.

To summarize, investment in DeFi funds offers the most passive and novice-friendly way to invest in DeFi assets. One example is Bitwise's DeFi Index F, which is one of the most popular indexes for tracking DeFi assets. They have low fees, low minimums, and easy access for novices. DeFi funds also provide exposure to new cryptocurrencies that can be traded on crypto exchanges. This allows investors to find coins they like without having to do any research on their own.

DeFi Risk and Rewards

The decentralized nature of the above-mentioned investments makes them particularly appealing to investors who are interested in the potential for high returns but also want the freedom to invest without the risk of losing their money.

DeFi is often compared to the investment opportunities available in the traditional finance sector, but there are some significant differences. One major difference is that DeFi investments are not traditionally regulated. This means that you can invest in a wide range of projects and companies, which can be both risky and rewarding.

The increased availability of these investments with little or no regulation means that there is an increased risk of losing money, but it also means that investors have more options to choose from. This provides an opportunity for investors who want to diversify their portfolios and for those who want to make a quick buck on the market without taking too much risk.

DeFi's growth accelerated in 2020, doubling from $700 million to $13 billion. Industry data from a variety of sources indicates that it may have reached $40 billion as of September 2021. These numbers show us that the potential of this new trend and form of investing is only growing, and it's not going to stop any time soon.

Some of the risks include:

- *DeFi is not yet regulated. There are still many uncertainties with the regulatory framework that will need to be addressed before this asset class can be fully embraced.*
- *Since there is a lack of regulation covering these investments, it is unclear what happens if an investor loses their funds. There are no guarantees that your investments will be safe.*
- *The price volatility of digital assets could lead to loss of value. The price of the digital asset or cryptocurrency can fluctuate, which potentially can quickly lead to losses.*
- *It is difficult to track the progress of an initial coin offering (ICO) or an obscure coin as they are often not listed on any exchange.*
- Many ICO projects are scams that do not have a working product and promise high returns without delivering.

Now that we know some of the potential risks of investing in DeFi, it is worth talking about the rewards that can be obtained by investing in this ecosystem.

Crypto investing has been a big trend in the last few years. The market has seen many ups and downs, but it is still growing. Investors are making their money back, and they are seeing good returns on their investments in the long term.

Investing in this space can be complicated for newbies. There are a lot of terms that you might not know about, like smart contracts, options, or ICOs. These terms can intimidate newbies and prevent them from investing in the space, but there are some great payoffs for those who take the plunge with DeFi and get involved early on.

Because of this, cryptocurrency has become a hot topic in the financial world. It is not only used as a payment method but also as an investment option, especially in the current digital age.

Some of the rewards of investing in the DeFi space are:

- *The risk for investors in DeFi funds are lower than traditional stocks or bonds because they are not directly tied to any company or country but rather to cryptocurrency itself. This means that investors cannot lose their money if they do not buy at the right time or sell too early.*
- *There is the potential to make money with a high ROI.*
- *It's possible to generate passive income.*
- *DeFi presents investors with an opportunity to diversify portfolios.*
- DeFi provides access to new opportunities that are not available in traditional markets.

Investing in DeFi can be a rewarding experience. Many people have profited from investing in cryptocurrencies like Bitcoin and Ether. These cryptocurrencies have seen huge returns (and losses) over short periods of time while increasing in value over the long haul and displaying potential for long-term growth. On top of that, investors can also make money with a high ROI by trading them on an exchange or using them as collateral for loans.

Despite the risks, investing in DeFi is a viable option if you are looking to invest in cryptocurrencies. The potential for making money with this type of investment has always been there and it is only now that inventors are realizing the opportunity it presents.

The reward for DeFi investors is the ability to make money by investing in assets that are not easily accessible to traditional investors. Investors should be careful with their investments and should keep track of what they invest in so they know what they are getting into.

7. The Success of Defi Is Achieved by Smart Contracts

There is no doubt that Smart Contracts have what it takes to disrupt industries like telecommunication, music, banking, film, insurance, education, and many others. The phrase "smart contract" is commonly used in the crypto space to describe a computer code that can facilitate the exchange of property, money, or other valuables.

Anytime the parties involved meet the predefined rules, the agreement will be automatically enforced. This is undoubtedly the smartest form of decentralized automation. Since they run on the blockchain, Smart Contracts operate as they're programmed to, and there is no possibility of downtime, fraud, censorship, or interference from a third party.

The truth is that all blockchains can process code; however, a good number of them are still limited, and this is where Ethereum differs. Instead of providing limited operations, the Ethereum platform offers developers the resources to build any application.

Here is a simple explanation of what Smart Contracts can do: individuals can exchange stock, money, property, and other assets without needing to engage the services of a lawyer. This significantly reduces the expensive third-party costs that are often incurred during such transactions. This is one of the reasons many people believe that Ethereum is superior to Bitcoin.

How Do Smart Contracts Work?

It starts with predefining the contract. At this point, all the terms of engagement are established by all stakeholders. This could be the specific currency used for making payments, the variable interest rate, or the currency rate. Also, the terms for execution are set while predefining the contract, and this could be the date, time, or several other criteria.

- **Events: this is where events (like the information received and the kick-off of the transaction) instantly trigger the implementation of the contract.**
- ***Execution and delivery:*** *they determine the movement of value. It also determines the terms of the contract based on the fulfillment of the set conditions*
- **Settlement of contract:** this is the final stage of the process, and it can take place in two ways. The first is off-chain assets, which means physical assets such as fiat and stocks. In this case, the changes to accounts on the distributed ledger will have to match the off-chain settlement instructions. The second type of settlement of contract

is on-chain, which has to do with digital assets. The accounts are automatically settled in the case of virtual assets like digital currency.

With Smart Contracts, to get the particular product you want, all you need to do is deposit the cryptocurrency required. The entire process is automated, so if a buyer or seller fails to fulfill their end of the bargain, the transactions will not be completed. The Ethereum Smart Contract will instantly cancel the transaction in the spirit of "if you don't comply."

The truth is Smart Contracts could be complex or simple contracts. A good example of simple Smart Contracts is the time-stamping services for an art registry. It can also be used by non-profits, governmental organizations, and semi-governmental organizations to maintain records. These could be records for schools, land titles, university degrees, and birth certificates.

On the other hand, several regulatory aspects make up complex contracts. One excellent example is the Decentralized Autonomous Organization, which is also one of the most complex Smart Contracts.

Advantages of Smart Contracts

Trust

With Smart Contracts, you won't lose your documents, and no one can steal them because they are encrypted and safely kept on a shared secured ledger. Also, with Smart Contracts, you don't need to trust the individuals you're dealing with from any location around the globe, and you shouldn't expect them to trust you either. The system is unbiased and effectively replaces trust.

Autonomy

There isn't a need for third parties or a facilitator, which gives you complete control of the agreement.

Safety

If Smart Contracts are implemented appropriately, they are very difficult to hack. Also, your documents will be safely stored by the environments for Smart Contracts, which are effectively protected with complex cryptography.

Savings

There isn't a need for advisors, estate agents, assistants, notaries, and other intermediaries. This also translates to a significant reduction in the exorbitant fees that come with their services.

Efficiency

The time you would normally waste processing documents and sending them to specific locations is saved when you use Smart Contracts.

Transparency

All relevant parties can easily access the terms and conditions of the contract. The moment an agreement has been established; it won't be disputed anymore.

Accuracy

A basic requirement for every Smart Contract is that all the terms and conditions of the contract should be recorded in detail. The reason for this is that a single omission can lead to transaction errors. This helps automated contracts avoid the pitfalls that are common with forms that are completed manually.

Clear Communication

I mentioned earlier that there is a need to record everything in detail. This is what ensures that there is no misinterpretation or miscommunication. Clear communication also helps eliminate the inefficiency associated with communication gaps.

Storage and Backup

During every transaction, Smart Contracts are also used to record important transactions. So, the details of all stakeholders are permanently stored when used in a contract. This helps for future reference, and in the event of data loss, the parties involved can retrieve the attributes of the contract.

Guaranteed Outcome

One of the reasons most people involved in transactions go to court is because one or more persons have failed to abide by the rules and terms of the agreement. But Smart Contracts can significantly lower or even eliminate the need for litigation. Parties will always be committed to operating by the rules of the underlying code when using self-executing contracts.

How to Buy Cryptocurrencies

Trading cryptocurrencies are all about a repeated process of buying and selling. However, you cannot just buy and sell cryptocurrencies at random. Every buy and sell order that you make should be made strategically and backed up with solid research. When buying and selling a cryptocurrency, it is important to note that there is a difference between the buy price and the selling price.

You will be glad to hear that purchasing these digital currencies is not difficult. But, you do need to have a good idea of what you are looking for. If you want to go with one of the more popular digital currencies, then the best exchange site to work with is Coinbase. Coinbase will allow investors to exchange Litecoin, Ethereum, and Bitcoin. There are many sites you can buy crypto, some of them includes:

- **Binance**
- *Bittrex*
- *Coinbase*
- *Cashapp*
- *Coin exchange*
- Jubiter.com

The buying price is always higher than the selling price. This is mainly how a broker earns a profit. Before you buy and sell any cryptocurrency be sure to do research to see the prevailing market rate for buying and selling.

A good way to do this is by viewing the rates as offered by different reputable brokers. You should also check the price of the cryptocurrency that you want to buy/sell on coinmarketcap and coingecko just to give you an idea of the prevailing rate. You may find some slight differences in the price also considering that the prices of the different cryptocurrencies in the market continuously fluctuate. Always remember the number one trading principle: buy low, sell high.

Selling is just as important as buying. Selling is where you finally close your position and turn your cryptocurrency into fiat money. Reputable cryptocurrency wallets like Coinbase will allow you to sell cryptocurrencies directly from your Coinbase wallet. If your wallet does not allow you to sell cryptocurrencies, then you should open a trading account with a trustworthy broker.

Contrary to what other people think, selling cryptocurrency also takes skill and strategy. It is not just about converting a cryptocurrency into cash, but it is also about proper timing. Any of these three things that can happen when you sell a cryptocurrency:

- **You are in a profit already, and you would like to sell your cryptocurrency to finally close your position and turn your profit into cash.**
- *You accepted your losses and would like to sell your cryptocurrency to avoid possible future losses.*
- You sell your cryptocurrency only to regret it when the price increases after selling.

Of course, there is also the lingering idea of not selling your cryptocurrency and hoping that its price will continuously increase. However, when you take this approach, you should also consider the risk that the price of the cryptocurrency concerned might suddenly drop. Again, do not underestimate the high volatility of the cryptocurrency market. As you can see, selling a cryptocurrency can also be quite complicated. There are things that you should consider. Before you sell your cryptocurrency, it is advised that you should first study the cryptocurrency market. The more that you understand the cryptocurrency market, especially the cryptocurrency that you intend to buy/sell, the more like that you can come up with the right trading decision. Keep in mind that you are dealing with a constantly moving and evolving market. You cannot just buy and sell cryptocurrencies at random. You must have the right understanding and apply an effective strategy to significantly increase your chances of making a profitable trade.

Purchase Risk

There is a risk that you face when you purchase coins from unknown sellers. Especially if you are doing it with fiats. There is a chance that once you pay for it, they do not transfer the coin. So that is a risk that you must contend with when you find a broker to purchase the coin and when you start trading. There are two strategies to overcome this. The first is that you can buy the coin from a reputable seller. That way you deposit the funds and the coins are certain to reach your wallet. From there you transfer the contents of your wallet to a hosted wallet with the trading broker. Then you can make whatever trades you want. That takes out the purchase risk. But you still have one more risk when it comes to trading.

What most people do not understand is that there are a number of trading houses out there that operate on the fringe. What they do is take your coin (be it BTC, Ethereum, or Monero) and they then make the purchase on the market or you. Sometimes, they do not make the actual purchase and they just record the ledger as the purchase being made. This happens a lot in all brokerages because one of the ways traditional financial brokers work is that they buy popular assets in bulk, keep some for themselves and their discretionary accounts, then apportion the rest out to other customers who also bought them.

This risk happens with new brokerages trying to make it in big in short order. When it comes to brokerages, you have to be smart. Either choose a brokerage that has been around for a while or one that provides you with the safeguards you demand.

Purchase and counterparty risk are very real in all trading environments, and the same applies to a larger degree in online cryptocurrency brokerages. The rule of thumb is that if you lose your money to a brokerage that goes upside down, you will never get your money. Be comfortable with that fact and place only what you need to with them at any one time. If you are going to be a heavy trader, then you need to set up the necessary infrastructure to cold-store the coins that are not in play. And since you should only be investing half of your coins (at the most) at any one time, or investing at two different brokerages who aren't related, then it becomes worth your time to set up an off-line storage that is air-gapped and secured.

8. Cryptocurrencies and Investing

There are some important questions to ask yourself before you invest in a cryptocurrency, and you've already read about some of them.

There are many factors to consider when determining the best cryptocurrency for you:

- *Is it a decentralized currency?*
- *What does it offer?*
- *What are its features?*
- How is it going to grow in the future?

Cryptocurrencies are relatively new and still evolving, so it is hard to predict the future of cryptocurrencies in general, never mind any one token. A lot of people have invested in cryptocurrencies, but there is no way to predict which cryptocurrency will perform best in the future. We can only hope that they will continue to evolve as a technology.

The best cryptocurrency is an important and relevant debate in the crypto community. There is no absolute answer. With that said, let's look at some of the most popular cryptocurrencies out there.

Bitcoin

As mentioned, Bitcoin is a digital currency that was created in 2009 by an unknown person or group of people under the name Satoshi Nakamoto. It uses cryptography to control its creation and transactions, and transactions are redundantly recorded in many decentralized nodes.

Bitcoin is that it is not controlled by any central authority, but instead operates on the principles of a peer-to-peer network. Network nodes verify transactions using cryptography, and transactions are recorded in a public ledger called the blockchain. The blockchain's data can be viewed online by anyone with an internet connection.

Bitcoin is special because it is the first digital currency to be created without any central authority or government backing. The Bitcoin blockchain can be used to send and receive money, but it has many other uses, too. In fact, you can use the blockchain to do almost anything you want, including verifying the authenticity of documents, voting on propositions, and even buying a house.

The maximum number of Bitcoins (BTC) that can ever exist in the market is capped at 21 million. There are already 17 million BTC in circulation. The reward for Bitcoin miners for each block added to the blockchain started at 50 BTC at the crypto currency's inception, and it halves after every 210,000 mined blocks, roughly every four years. The last halving took place in May 2020, and that reduced the reward per block to 6.25 BTC. Once all 21 million BTC have been created, miners will instead earn fees from transactions.

Ethereum

Ethereum is a blockchain-based platform with its own cryptocurrency called Ether (ETH). It was proposed in late 2013 by Vitalik Buterin and was released on July 30, 2015. Ethereum is the most popular decentralized platform for creating applications and since its inception has grown to become the second largest cryptocurrency after Bitcoin.

The Ethereum platform is open-source, meaning anyone can download the software and contribute to the project. The platform has been widely adopted for smart contracts, which are self-enforcing digital agreements that run on the blockchain.

As it is a blockchain-based platform, Ethereum allows users to make direct peer-to-peer agreements and transactions without the need for third-party intermediaries. Ether, on the other hand, is the native token of Ethereum that people trade in and it has its own unique properties.

Ether is a digital token that can be transferred between accounts and also used to pay for transactions on the network. It has become an asset of significant value, with its price fluctuating similarly to other cryptocurrencies.

It is important to understand that Ethereum is more than just a cryptocurrency. It is an entire platform that facilitates the development of decentralized applications (DApps) and smart contracts, which can be used to build advanced business processes. It aims to create blockchain-based businesses and make transactions simpler, faster, and more secure.

Another interesting thing is that developers can use Ethereum to create and issue digital items within the decentralized Ethereum network. It definitely has the potential to revolutionize the world of technology and ultimately change the world for the better.

The public generally trusts Ethereum more than it does Bitcoin, largely because its developers do not hide behind pseudonyms like Bitcoin's Satoshi Nakamoto.

The programming language that developers use to build on Ethereum is called Solidarity. It is a programming language with an emphasis on security and safety. It has the ability to write programs without any human intervention, making it more secure than competing programming languages like Python or Java.

Solidarity was designed for the Ethereum network, so it has a lot of features that make it more adapted than other languages to that environment. One of these features is that Solidarity can be run by anyone in the world, which means no one can control its development or usage. At the same time, Solidarity allows developers to create their own cryptocurrency and DApps without downtime, fraud, regulation, or intermediaries.

Ethereum is not bound by total supply limits like BTC. There is only one limit to Ethereum mining: only 18 million ETH can be mined annually. Some people expect that ETH will overtake BTC and become the most popular cryptocurrency in the world.

Ethereum is also faster than Bitcoin. Bitcoin can only handle up to 4.6 transactions per second while Ethereum can process up to 15 transactions per second. This means that Ethereum can be used as a much more efficient payment system than Bitcoin or any other cryptocurrency out there.

Ethereum currently also has a faster mining rate than Bitcoin. When it began, mining and proof of work were the critical technologies. But Ethereum has shifted to adopt proof of stake, which requires less power consumption than proof of work and Ethereum is more environmentally friendly than Bitcoin because it. The shift from proof of work to proof of stake is also beneficial because it allows Ethereum's blockchain to scale in a much smoother way than Bitcoin's blockchain could ever do.

Ethereum has been one of the most popular cryptocurrencies in the market. It has a robust business case and is considered to be one of the most valuable cryptocurrencies. But that is not the end of it. There are many more exciting things on the horizon for Ethereum, which will make it even more valuable in future years.

Litecoin

Litecoin is a peer-to-peer cryptocurrency that was designed to be a faster, cheaper, and more reliable form of payment than Bitcoin. In the past few years, the price of Litecoin has consistently grown, putting it in the top-10 most-valuable cryptocurrencies.

It was introduced in 2011 by Charlie Lee, a computer scientist, former Google employee, and MIT graduate. Its aim was to create a more accessible and cheaper version of Bitcoin. It enables instant payments to anyone in the world and can be used for low-cost or even free transactions.

Litecoin was one of the very first altcoins on the market. Many altcoins appeared between 2011 and 2013, and many altcoins have since disappeared. However, Litecoin continues to be a popular cryptocurrency. Litecoin is an open-source project, so anyone can download the software for free and start mining it on their own computer. In this respect, Litecoin is more accessible than Bitcoin, which requires robust, expensive hardware to mine for profit.

Litecoin is largely considered as Bitcoin's little brother but it has some fundamental differences. For example, it is faster and more effective than Bitcoin, meaning that it generates blocks faster. A Litecoin block generates every 2.5 minutes on average compared to the 10 minutes of a Bitcoin block.

Litecoin transactions cost less in fees and use Scrypt for encryption instead of the SHA-256 algorithm that Bitcoin does. Litecoin is less expensive than Bitcoin by design. With its lower mining fees, it can handle more transactions per second and it is easier for people to use and cheaper for businesses to accept.

All of these features make Litecoin a unique and more accessible cryptocurrency for those who do not want to deal with the complexity of Bitcoin. Litecoin is a popular cryptocurrency, one of the most successful in its short existence.

Ripple

Ripple is a payment protocol that has been around since 2012 and is now also used by many financial institutions as an alternative to traditional currencies. It was created by business executive and angel investor Chris Larsen, and entrepreneur, programmer, and philanthropist Jed McCaleb. Ripple's goal is to provide a global settlement network for the world's financial transactions, which will allow for low-cost, reliable, real-time payment systems.

Ripple is an open-source software that allows banks to send international payments at low cost, in real time, without the need for pre-funded nostro accounts (a nostro account is a foreign currency account that a bank holds).

Ripple's blockchain-powered protocol is designed to process 1,500 transactions per second with no charge for the sender or receiver. In practice, the average Ripple transaction process lasts five seconds, which makes it the fastest payment network in the world. Its transactions are also more transparent than traditional methods.

This technology has the potential to change the way banks do business and so far, more than 100 banks and financial institutions across the world have adopted the Ripple protocol. It provides fast, cheap, and convenient cross-border transactions and is an option for financial institutions that are looking for a cheaper way to do business internationally. It is an alternative to the current international payments system that most banks use, SWIFT.

So, Ripple is a company that provides a payment system and currency exchange. It is not a cryptocurrency as such, but it does have its own token called XRP. The XRP token can be used to make payments on the Ripple network.

The Ripple network uses a consensus algorithm that allows all parties involved to agree on the state of the ledger at any given time. This gives users complete control over their funds, while still allowing the transfer of funds with ease and speed.

Each transaction costs 0.00001 XRP, which even at the token's all-time high price was less than a fraction of a cent. This low transaction fee is definitely one of the things that makes Ripple so attractive to use for cross-border payments and remittances.

The XRP cryptocurrency is also used as a bridge currency. This means that it can be used to convert any other currency into XRP and then back into the original currency and it enables financial institutions to trade currencies more cheaply than ever before. XRP is the fastest, most-scalable digital asset currently available and it is also the only cryptocurrency with an established banking relationship.

In order for a cryptocurrency to be considered valid, it must have a consensus protocol. The XRP cryptocurrency uses a consensus protocol to verify transactions. Validators compare proposed transactions to the most recent ledger and if they are different, they reject the transaction and send it back for review.

One of the key differences between Ripple and Bitcoin is the supply of coins. The supply of Bitcoin is limited to 21 million coins, while the supply of XRP is limited to 100 billion coins. That's one reason that the price of a BTC is much higher than that of XRP.

Another difference is that although the XRP cryptocurrency is decentralized and not tied to any company, it still comes from a private company. That makes it centralized, unlike other cryptocurrencies such as Bitcoin or Ethereum. Many investors are not concerned about the relationship between Ripple and XRP, but some crypto enthusiasts view it as a negative thing. This has led to a lot of criticism from the crypto community because they do not agree that cryptocurrency should be managed by a private company or should have a centralized nature.

Some people believe that the XRP currency will not last long, and it will be replaced by a decentralized cryptocurrency in the future.

Despite all this controversy, there is no doubt Ripple has potential. Ripple has been able to disrupt the global financial system in multiple ways. One of the most important ways it has done so is by replacing an outdated and inefficient system for international money transfers with its own blockchain platform.

Ripple has partnerships with banks and financial institutions to help them adopt the blockchain technology. It is a promising sign that banks are willing to adopt the technology in order to stay relevant, which confirms the importance of cryptocurrencies and how they are gradually becoming an essential part of our daily lives.

Fraud and Scams Involving Cryptocurrency

Cryptocurrency fraud is a general term for the attempt to gain crypto tokens or assets by illegal means. Scams are a kind of cryptocurrency fraud, schemes that target people who have invested in cryptocurrencies.

Cryptocurrency scams can also be called Ponzi schemes, pyramid schemes, and get-rich-quick schemes as they promise to make their investors rich overnight. These scams usually promise high returns on investments at very low risk.

Cryptocurrency scams are a growing problem for cryptocurrency users. It can take many forms, such as getting someone to buy fake coins, getting them to send money to the wrong crypto wallet, or asking for payment in exchange for something that doesn't exist.

The most common form of cryptocurrency fraud is getting people to send money in exchange for something that doesn't exist. It could be anything from a bogus ICO to a fake crypto-wallet or even an empty wallet with no coins in it. The scammers make up false information about the project and ask you to invest in it so they can build it and promise to give you your share when they are done.

There is another type of crypto scam that involves fake sales pitches for individual retirement accounts in cryptocurrencies like Bitcoin or Ethereum.

Cryptocurrency scams have become a serious problem on the internet, which has led to many companies being sued for fraud. Here are some things to watch out for.

Fake Websites

With the increasing popularity of cryptocurrencies, more and more scammers are trying to get a piece of the pie by creating fake websites that offer huge and guaranteed returns.

These websites often look legitimate. They may display fake testimonials or awards. The testimonials are often written in a way that makes it sound like they are coming from real people who have experienced success with the product or service.

Virtual Ponzi Schemes

Ponzi schemes are scams that reward old investors with funds that new investors have paid into the investment. Another term for this is a pyramid scheme.

Virtual Ponzi schemes are scams that use the promise of high returns to lure investors. They are often connected to cryptocurrency and are very popular in the digital world.

Virtual Ponzi schemes have been around for a while but they have become more popular recently due to the huge rise in cryptocurrency value. In 2018, there were over 1,000 cases of virtual Ponzi schemes and this number is expected to grow over the next few years.

The most common way these scams work is by asking investors to buy into a certain coin or project. However, this strategy doesn't always work as intended, and victims lose their money as the scheme collapses.

Celebrity Endorsements

Cryptocurrency criminals use fake websites and social media accounts to promote non-existent opportunities to invest in digital currencies. They advertise these opportunities with the help of fake testimonials and images—and who is more convincing than a celebrity?

Scammers pose online as famous people who offer investment opportunities in cryptocurrency. This is a tactic that has been used for years, but it's becoming more popular now with the rise of cryptocurrencies.

It is important to be wary of such offers as there is no guarantee that the person you are speaking to actually has any connection to the celebrity they claim to be.

Legitimate companies and individuals often use celebrity endorsements to promote their product or service. Celebrities can offer a sense of trustworthiness and authenticity that people want in their endorsement. But maybe you shouldn't be taking investment advice from them.

Romance Scams

These types of scams are on the rise, with the FBI warning of a new trend where tricksters persuade people they meet on dating apps or social media to send cryptocurrency. Sometimes, the scammer claims to have a relative who is a trader and who can provide inside advice.

The FBI says that these scams have been around for a while, but these tricksters have flooded dating apps and other social media to befriend victims and persuade them to send cryptocurrency to their scam operation.

To provide some context about this serious issue, there were more than 1,800 reports of crypto-focused romance scams handled by the FBI's Internet Crime Complaint Center in the first seven months of 2021, with losses exceeding $133 million.

In order to avoid getting scammed, investors should always be cautious when they see anything related to digital currencies online. They should also use cryptocurrency tools like Google Trends or CoinMarketCap to verify if the website they are visiting is legitimate.

Is Cryptocurrency Safe?

The cryptocurrency market is highly volatile and risky. The cryptocurrency market has grown exponentially over the last few years with many people entering the market without understanding how it works or what it entails. There are many scams in the cryptocurrency world, but there are also some coins that you can trust.

Cryptocurrency scams are not hard to find. You should be careful when investing in cryptocurrencies and make sure to do your research before making any transactions.

While cryptocurrencies are built on blockchain technology and blockchains have so far proven safe from any form of manipulation or fraud. For the most part, cryptocurrency is safe. It requires two factors of authentication to conduct transactions. A username and password may be required before funds can be sent to your wallet, for instance—although there have been concerns about the security of cryptocurrency wallets.

Investing in cryptocurrency does carry some risks. Virtual currencies are solely influenced by supply and demand, which makes them inherently volatile. This makes it difficult for people to understand the value of cryptocurrencies and whether they are safe or not. The decentralized nature of cryptocurrency makes it hard to track and regulate, which has led to wild swings in price that can produce huge profits or losses for investors. It is a decision to consider.

Conclusion

You've taken in a lot of information in the course of reading this book! Hopefully now you feel more confident in your understanding of decentralized finance as well as how you can make money from it today. DeFi has the potential to remake not only finance, but other fields that use the same technology in the future.

Like other fields, DeFi has a lot of its own jargon: blockchain, cryptocurrency, miners, blocks, and so on. Now that you know what all these words mean or are in reference to, you're able to read other articles about the subject and discuss them intelligently. While the DeFi world started off mostly as cryptocurrency (namely Bitcoin), it's taken off since then. Currently, it's already more than just an alternative currency, and it has a lot of future potential.

You learned how the blockchain works, and why it's so secure. Though some thefts have occurred due to other weaknesses in the system, it's very difficult to hack into the blockchain and change something. That kind of fraud is rare, which is one of the reasons DeFi is so popular.

The distributed ledger of blockchain and DeFi also provides more transparency and transactions are easier to trace through history. Though individuals are anonymous, where the money or transaction has gone also makes fraud detection easier.

The decentralized world operates without a lot of human intermediaries and makes use of computer algorithms in smart contracts. As a result, the cost for financial services on the blockchain is much lower, and can potentially bring in millions of users who can't afford the fees of the traditional system.

Armed with this knowledge, you can choose to interact with the DeFi ecosystem however you want.

For that, I congratulate you and wish you all the best in your crypto journey.

If you enjoyed this book, please make sure to leave some great reviews, thank you.

www.ingramcontent.com/pod-product-compliance
Lightning Source LLC
LaVergne TN
LVHW082359200926
848481LV00012B/3621